THE ROAD TRAVELED
AND OTHER ESSAYS

THE ROAD TRAVELED
AND OTHER ESSAYS

Steven M. Cahn

RESOURCE *Publications* • Eugene, Oregon

THE ROAD TRAVELED AND OTHER ESSAYS

Resource Publications
An Imprint of Wipf and Stock Publishers
199 W. 8th Ave., Suite 3
Eugene, OR 97401

www.wipfandstock.com

PAPERBACK ISBN: 978-1-5326-6450-2
HARDCOVER ISBN: 978-1-5326-6451-9
EBOOK ISBN: 978-1-5326-6452-6

Manufactured in the U.S.A.   02/07/19

In tribute to

Leon Bramson

George F. Farr, Jr.

Geoffrey Marshall

CONTENTS

PREFACE

THE WRITINGS IN THIS collection, apart from the final article, were published within the past five years. A majority appeared on the blog of the APA (American Philosophical Association) or in *Think: Philosophy for Everyone*, a journal sponsored by the Royal Institute of Philosophy. In the title essay, which appears for the first time, the reader can learn about those to whom this volume is dedicated as well as others to whom I owe so much.

The essays in Part I concern well-being and present a line of argument I developed with Christine Vitrano, Associate Professor of Philosophy at Brooklyn College of The City University of New York. For elaboration, see our book *Happiness and Goodness: Philosophical Reflections on Living Well* (New York: Columbia University Press, 2015).

The essays in Part II form an essential part of my outlook on religious belief. A fuller presentation of my overall position can be found in my *Religion Within Reason* (New York: Columbia University Press, 2017).

The essays in Parts III and IV reflect my philosophy of higher education, a subject to which I have devoted much attention over decades. Further reflections on the subject are found in my *Saints and Scamps: Ethics in Academia*, 25th Anniversary Edition (Lanham, MD: Rowman & Littlefield, 2011); *From Student to Scholar: A Candid Guide to Becoming a Professor* (New York: Columbia University Press, 2008); *Teaching Philosophy: A Guide* (New York: Routledge, 2018), and *Inside Academia: Professors, Politics, and*

Policies (New Brunswick: Rutgers University Press, 2019). My earlier works on the subject, *The Eclipse of Excellence* (1973), *Scholars Who Teach: The Art of College Teaching* (1978), and *Education and the Democratic Ideal* (1979) were reprinted in 2004 by Wipf & Stock Publishers.

The puzzles in Part V generated responses in the sources where they appeared. I hope readers will find these conundrums provocative.

In the autobiographical essay that concludes the book, I refer to Richard Taylor's argument for fatalism and the paper I wrote in its defense. These can be found in Steven M. Cahn and Maureen Eckert, eds., *Fate, Time, and Language: An Essay on Free Will by David Foster Wallace* (New York: Columbia University Press, 2011). My overall assessment of fatalism is presented in my *Fate, Logic, and Time* (New Haven: Yale University Press, 1967), reprinted in 2004 by Wipf & Stock Publishers.

Two previous collections of my papers are *Philosophical Explorations: Freedom, God, and Goodness* (Amherst, NY: Prometheus Books, 1989) and *Puzzles & Perplexities: Collected Essays*, Second Edition (Lanham, MD: Lexington Books, 2007).

For a comprehensive list of my authored and edited books as of 2018, see *Teaching Philosophy: A Guide*.

PART I

WELL-BEING

1

LIVING WELL

co-authored with Christine Vitrano

IN RONALD DWORKIN'S POSTHUMOUSLY published *Religion Without God*, he argues that an atheist can be religious. While this claim would come as no surprise to adherents of Jainism, Theravada Buddhism, or Mimamsa Hinduism, Dworkin has in mind not these Asian religious traditions but a viewpoint common to many Western thinkers denying theism yet recognizing "nature's intrinsic beauty" and the "inescapable responsibility" of each person to "live well."[1] Dworkin considers such an outlook religious.

Leaving aside his curious line of thought that finds support for religious belief in such disparate phenomena as the Grand Canyon, the prowling of jaguars, and the discovery by physicists of the Higgs boson, let us concentrate instead on his view that we should all seek to live well so as to achieve "successful" lives and avoid "wasted" ones.[2]

Does one model fit all? On this important point Dworkin wavers. He maintains that "there is, independently and objectively, a right way to live." Yet he also recognizes "the responsibility of each

1. Dworkin, *Religion Without God*, 2, 4, 155.
2. Dworkin, *Religion Without God*, 10, 2.

person to decide for himself ethical questions about which kinds of lives are appropriate and which would be degrading for him."[3]

What sort of life did Dworkin find degrading? We are not told but suspect that for such a successful academic, a degrading life might have been one without intellectual striving, just as a famed athlete might find to be degrading a life as a couch potato.

But what sorts of lives are worthy? To help answer the question, consider the following two fictional, though realistic, cases.

I. Pat received a bachelor's degree from a prestigious college, earned a PhD in philosophy from a leading university, was awarded an academic position at a first-rate school, and eventually earned tenure there. Pat is the author of numerous books, articles, and reviews, is widely regarded as a leading scholar and teacher, and is admired by colleagues and students for fairness and helpfulness. Pat is happily married, has two children, enjoys playing bridge and the cello, and vacations each summer in a modest house on Cape Cod. Physically and mentally healthy, Pat is in good spirits, looking forward to years of continued happiness.

II. Lee did not attend college. After graduation from high school, Lee moved to a beach community in California and is devoted to sunbathing, swimming, and surfing. Lee has never married but has experienced numerous romances. Having inherited wealth from deceased parents, Lee has no financial needs but, while donating generously to worthy causes, spends money freely on magnificent homes, luxury cars, the latest in electronic equipment, designer clothes, meals in fine restaurants, golfing holidays, and trips to far-flung locations. Lee has many friends and is admired for honesty and kindness. Physically and mentally healthy, Lee is in good spirits, looking forward to years of continued happiness.

Both Pat and Lee live in ways that appear to suit them. Both enjoy prosperity, treat others with respect, engage in activities they

---

3. Dworkin, *Religion Without God*, 155, 114.

find fulfilling, and report they are happy. So are both living well? Are both pursuing equally successful lives? Is either life being wasted?

Dworkin offers little guidance to help answer these questions. He urges that we "make our lives into works of art,"[4] but works of art typically contain complexities and conflicts not found in the lives of Pat or Lee. The story of each might be told in the form of a play or novel, but neither individual appears to have the makings of a Medea, Hamlet, or Raskolnikov.

Dworkin remarks that "Someone creates a work of art from his life if he lives and loves well in family or community with no fame or artistic achievement at all."[5] Here Dworkin, having urged us to live well by making our lives into works of art, unhelpfully explains that works of art are those made by living well. This circular explanation sheds no light on how to live well, so Dworkin's appeal to works of art does not help us choose between the lives of Pat and Lee.

Many other philosophers, however, have provided reasons for believing that Pat's life is superior to Lee's. They rate the pursuit of philosophical inquiry, playing the cello, or raising a family more highly than surfing, having a series of romances, or living in a luxurious home.

Yet not all philosophers agree with this assessment. Two who do not are Richard Taylor and Harry Frankfurt, each of whom would maintain that Pat and Lee are living equally well.

Consider first Taylor's approach. He discusses the case of Sisyphus, who, according to Greek myth, was condemned for his misdeeds to the eternal task of rolling a huge stone to the top of a hill, only each time to have it roll down to the bottom again. Is the activity of Sisyphus meaningless? Taylor concludes that the answer depends on whether Sisyphus has a desire to roll stones up hills. Most of us don't, but if Sisyphus does, then he has found "mission and meaning."[6] So, according to Taylor, living well is living in

---

4. Dworkin, *Religion Without God*, 157–58.

5. Dworkin, *Religion Without God*, 158.

6. Taylor, *Good and Evil*, 324.

accord with your desires. If your activities match your wishes, then your life is successful. Whether the activity is teaching philosophy, driving luxury cars, or rolling stones up hills makes no difference.

Frankfurt reaches a similar conclusion. He maintains that we infuse our lives with meaning by loving certain intrinsic ends and caring about the means to achieve them. Need they be of a particular sort? Not according to Frankfurt. As he writes, "Devoting oneself to what one loves suffices to make one's life meaningful, regardless of the inherent or objective character of the objects that are loved."[7] Therefore while Pat loves discussing philosophy, playing bridge, and spending time with family, Lee loves surfing, golfing, and engaging in romantic adventures. Thus, according to Frankfurt, both possess the essentials of a meaningful life.

As we noted, however, most philosophers reject this view of what makes a life significant.[8] Susan Wolf, for instance, argues that if your life is to have meaning, you need to be engaged with projects of worth, i.e., those with objective value.[9] What are these? Unfortunately, Wolf offers no theory of objective value to guide us, but she does provide examples of activities that are worthwhile and others that are not. For example, she maintains that caring for an ailing friend gives life meaning but providing financial support for a sick stranger does not; practicing a religion gives life meaning but playing computer games does not; climbing a mountain gives life meaning but solving crossword puzzles does not.

How about a life devoted exclusively to the practice of corporate law? Is that more akin to climbing a mountain or solving crossword puzzles? Wolf isn't sure and declares the matter controversial. Whether her assessment would be different if the legal specialty were, for example, constitutional law is not clear.

Nevertheless, we might suppose that Wolf would look with greater favor on Pat's interests than Lee's. But perhaps not.

7. Frankfurt, "Reply to Susan Wolf," 250.

8. See, for example, Darwall, *Welfare and Rational Care*; Kraut, *What is Good and Why*; and Wolf, *Meaning in Life*.

9. Wolf, *Meaning in Life*, 34–39.

Consider her reply to psychologist Jonathan Haidt, who suspects that Wolf's list of meaningful activities presupposes "*politically liberal* bourgeois American values." As a challenge to her views, he presents the case of one of his students, a shy woman who was passionate about horses: riding them, studying their history, and making "horse friends" with others who shared her passion. Haidt argues that this woman found meaning in life through her interest in horses, but he recognizes that "all of her horsing around does nothing for anyone else, and it does not make the world a better place."[10] So according to Haidt, Wolf's theory of objective value fails in this case.

In replying to Haidt, however, Wolf takes a surprising step. Rather than dismissing horses as an appropriate subject on which to build a worthwhile life, Wolf emphasizes that you need not accept someone else's word for what has objective value, then suggests that horses might well contribute to the meaningfulness of the woman's life, and concludes that a person's liking some activity, whatever it may be, can lead to its becoming valuable for that individual. What, then, becomes of objective value? Wolf senses the problem and admits that her discussion "may leave others either disappointed by what they see as watering down of what is distinctive about my conception of meaningfulness, or confused about what the point of it is, if it is to be understood so broadly."[11] We share such confusion.

If we follow Wolf's line of reasoning about the case of the woman who loved horses, then Lee's life might be on a par with Pat's. After all, if riding horses makes a life worthwhile, why not swimming, driving luxury cars, and traveling to far-flung locations?

Perhaps Wolf goes astray in formulating her list of worthwhile activities, so let us consider the list offered by Richard Kraut, who maintains that "a flourishing human being is one who possesses, develops, and enjoys the exercise of cognitive, affective, sensory,

---

10. Haidt, "Comment," 96–97.

11. Wolf, *Meaning in Life*, 131.

and social powers (no less than physical powers)."[12] Does this description fit Pat better than Lee?

Kraut probably would suppose so, but the answer is not obvious. Consider the following activities he cites with approval: playing tennis, writing poetry, cooking, running an organization, philosophizing, and enjoying our sexual powers. Here are some other activities Kraut finds of lesser value: bowling, playing checkers, accumulating wealth, achieving fame, holding socially isolating jobs, and remaining single.

As with Wolf's list, Kraut's raises more questions than it answers. Why is tennis better than bowling? How do both compare to badminton, archery, or quoits? Why is cooking better than checkers? How do both compare to gardening, hiking, or playing Monopoly? What's the matter with socially isolating jobs, such as serving as a lighthouse keeper, exploring a rain forest, writing fiction in a remote cabin, or doing research in a library cubicle? Why are fame and wealth denigrated, when most of us, including philosophy professors, are motivated by the possibility of receiving increased recognition and higher salaries? Furthermore, why does the study of philosophy invariably appear on philosophers' lists of worthwhile activities, whereas the study of such subjects as sociology, geology, Asian religions, ceramics, and finance are rarely cited with enthusiasm?

Perhaps surprisingly, Kraut's criteria for flourishing might well fit Lee's life: Lee's surfing would presumably lead to greater development of physical powers, Lee's travel might offer a wider perspective on understanding the world, Lee's many friends might offer a richer social life, and Lee's romances might lead to significant development of affective and sexual powers. How are we to weigh these advantages against Pat's devotion to research, teaching, family, and hobbies? The answer is unclear, but if Kraut's criteria do not favor the life of Pat or Lee, what guidance do they provide for living well? In any case, they would be especially unconvincing to an unmarried person who belongs to a bowling league.

---

12. Kraut, *What is Good and Why*, 137.

Assuming that lists of more and less worthwhile activities offer too easy a target for criticism, why not avoid specifics and simply assert that living well is pursuing goals of intrinsic value? That strategy is adopted by Stephen Darwall, who claims that "the best life for human beings is one of significant engagement in activities through which we come into appreciative rapport with agent-neutral values, such as aesthetic beauty, knowledge and understanding, and the worth of living beings."[13] Darwall here fails to take into account John Dewey's insight that any good may be viewed as of intrinsic worth and not a means to something else: "We can imagine a man who at one time thoroughly enjoys converse with his friends; at another the hearing of a symphony; at another the eating of his meals; at another the reading of a book; at another the earning of money, and so on. As an appreciative realization, each of these is an intrinsic value. It occupies a particular place in life; it serves its own end, which cannot be supplied by a substitute."[14] Thus sometimes Pat considers philosophy, bridge, or playing the cello to have intrinsic value, while Lee thinks the same of surfing, golf, or travel.

Darwall, however, adds that our activities are meritorious only if others recognize them as such. We should, therefore, focus on "things that matter," and things matter only if others who care about us judge that our choices "have worth."[15] Do Pat's friends find Pat's life to be of worth? Quite likely. Do Lee's friends find Lee's life to be of worth? Also quite likely. Thus we have reached an impasse.

To illustrate the problem more vividly, consider the real-life case of Phil Saltman, a jazz pianist in the 1930s and 1940s, whose extraordinary talents could have propelled him to international renown.[16] But after appearing as soloist with the Boston Pops Orchestra, he decided that life as a touring musician was not to his liking, and he chose instead to open a summer music camp for

---

13. Darwall, *Welfare and Rational Care*, 75.

14. Boydston, *Middle Works of John Dewey*, 247.

15. Darwall, *Welfare and Rational Care*, 95, 97.

16. See his *Method of Modern Jazz*.

boys and girls who enjoyed playing music, even if they did not plan to pursue the activity professionally. The camp flourished,[17] and he never doubted his choice to give up the opportunity for a distinguished solo career in order to guide youngsters and play music with them in amateur combos. Did he make a mistake? Did he limit his chances for a successful life? Did he waste his most significant talents? Some of his friends thought so; others did not. Thus Darwall's test is unhelpful. Regardless, why should Phil Saltman's friends have been given the final say? They probably did not fully understand his situation, and in any case the life at stake was his, not theirs.

We should also note that like Wolf and Kraut, Darwall takes philosophy as a paradigm case of a worthwhile activity. As he puts it, "Readers of this essay might agree that philosophy and philosophical activity have intrinsic worth."[18]

No doubt most would. Keep in mind, however, the insightful words of the pre-Socratic philosopher Xenophanes, who is said to have remarked that "if oxen and horses and lions had hands, and could draw with their hands and do what man can do, horses would draw the gods in the shape of horses, and oxen in the shape of oxen, each giving the gods bodies similar to their own."[19]

Of course, most philosophers find philosophy to be worthwhile, just as most chess players find chess to be worthwhile. After all, how many of us suppose that a successful life depends on engaging in activities that we do not enjoy or may hardly understand? Instead, we are prone to urge others to recognize the worth of at least some of our preferred undertakings. For instance, rarely do philosophers fight fires, achieve extraordinary feats of athleticism, or amass large sums of money in business ventures. Few philosophers, therefore, are apt to find as much value in firefighting, professional sports, or commerce as in contemplation.

---

17. Known as Camp Encore/Coda, it continues under the directorship of Phil Saltman's son and daughter-in-law; its history can be found at *www.encore-coda.com.*

18. Darwall, *Welfare and Rational Care*, 79.

19. Robinson, *Introduction to Early Greek Philosophy*, 52.

The high regard in which philosophers hold philosophy, an attitude historically associated with Aristotle,[20] has been expressed recently by Neil Levy. He argues that the best of all lives is the pursuit of knowledge, exemplified most clearly in philosophical inquiry, which to his mind is an activity open only to "an elite" fortunate enough to possess "cognitive abilities, of a special sort, which are. . .extremely sophisticated *relative* to the population norm."[21] The supposition that academics, especially philosophers, are more intelligent than all others is not likely to survive witnessing even one faculty meeting. Nevertheless, Levy is committed to the view that work as a physician, judge, business executive, airline pilot, violinist, electrician, caregiver, or parent ranks below spending countless hours assessing such matters as proposed solutions to the Gettier problem. We find this implication to be a *reductio ad absurdum* of his position.

Now let us return to assessing the lives of Pat and Lee. While we reject the assumption that for all people at all times certain activities are intrinsically worthier than others, we nevertheless note two crucial ways in which Pat and Lee are alike. Despite the vast differences in their interests, both act morally, neither harming anyone. How could they be living well while behaving unethically? To speak, as Frankfurt does, of Nazism offering its leaders a "complex, exhilarating, and rewarding life" is unconvincing.[22] Value cannot be found in doing unmitigated evil. Nor, as Taylor apparently overlooks, can the desire to act immorally provide the basis for living well.

But Pat and Lee not only act ethically; both are also happy. They have found deep satisfaction in their respective lives. Granted, we might urge either one to consider alternatives. Perhaps we could suggest to Lee the study of philosophy, lauding its power to

---

20. The *locus classicus* is Book X of the *Nicomachean Ethics*, trans. David Ross, rev. J. L. Ackrill and J. O Urmson (Oxford: Oxford University Press, 1998), where at 1178a5 Aristotle maintains that a life of contemplation is "best and pleasantest."

21. Levy, "Downshifting and Meaning in Life," 187–188.

22. Frankfurt, "Reply to Susan Wolf," 247.

help understand the human condition. Lee might take our suggestion and find philosophy fascinating; then again, Lee might find it opaque and boring. Likewise, perhaps we could urge Pat to take up golf. Pat might enjoy it, or, contrary to our expectations, consider it a waste of time. We can offer such suggestions to both of them, but doing so doesn't imply that the life of either is in any way unsatisfactory.

Suppose, however, that Pat and Lee were fundamentally frustrated or angry. Suppose they regretted many important decisions they had made, resented how they were treated by others, or rued what they considered to be a long series of misfortunes. Under those circumstances, even if their actions had been socially beneficial, the results for them would have been negative.

Our view, then, is that acting morally and finding long-term satisfaction are necessary conditions for living well. Seeing no plausible case for any other, we consider them jointly sufficient. By that standard, Pat and Lee both are living well. We might admire the life of one more than the other, but such a judgment would reflect our own preferences or purposes and not provide an appropriate basis for determining whose life is well-lived.

In conclusion, let us return to Ronald Dworkin's account of a religious outlook, which he took to include belief in a world where "objective value permeates everything," and human beings should act in accord with "life's intrinsic meaning."[23]

We do not share his view, but neither do some notable religious thinkers. Consider, for example, the author of the Book of Ecclesiastes, who declares that "everything is futile and pursuit of wind."[24] How, then, are we to act? The answer provided is brief and blunt: "There is nothing worthwhile for a man but to eat and drink and afford himself enjoyment with his means."[25]

23. Dworkin, *Religion Without God*, 1, 11.

24. Eccl 2:17. The translation is from *Tanakh: The Holy Scriptures* (Philadelphia: Jewish Publication Society, 1968).

25. Eccl 2:24.

This position is properly understood as applying only within the bounds of morality[26] and not sanctioning the foolish pursuit of unrestrained pleasures.[27] Even so, Dworkin would surely have judged the outlook misguided. We, on the contrary, find it astute.

POSTSCRIPT

Max Loxterkamp[28] correctly attributes to us the view that people are living well if they act morally and find long-term satisfaction, regardless of the pursuits they choose. He disagrees with us, however, and suggests that lives are better if they benefit society, and he offers as examples a charity worker, a courageous soldier, and a philosopher of genius.

Nevertheless, the question that concerns us is not whose life is more useful to others. If importance to the life of the community were the criterion for living well, few would rank above those who maintain piping for water, repair electrical equipment, make goods from raw materials, and grow and prepare food. Life will go on in the temporary absence of philosophers, but could we survive even a month without plumbers, electricians, and those who labor on farms, in factories, or in kitchens? Are the lives of such workers better than those of philosophers? We don't believe so. And what of philosophers whose writings attract little, if any, attention? Are they failing to live well? Again, we don't believe so. For such reasons, we do not judge living well in terms of meeting societal needs.

As to Loxtercamp's concern that we do not defend a specific moral theory, we assume that any moral person cares about others, treats them with respect, and seeks to minimize their suffering. So long as a person acts in this way (even if not going beyond the call of duty), whether that person is living well depends on the person's finding long-term satisfaction.

26. Eccl 7:17.
27. Eccl 10:17.
28. Loxterkamp, "Morality, Objective Value."

We criticize the views of Ronald Dworkin, Susan Wolf, Richard Kraut, and Stephen Darwall for not providing criteria for a good life that enable us to distinguish those who live well from those who don't. The problem we see is not, as Loxterkamp supposes, that the theories of these philosophers cannot resolve hard cases; rather, they cannot consistently resolve simple cases. If riding horses can make a life worthwhile, what activities, if any, would not make a life worthwhile?

Incidentally, the individuals whose cases we discuss in detail are named "Pat" and "Lee." Loxterkamp assumes they are male. We make no such assumption.

2

The Variety of Good Lives

Suppose a person I shall call Leslie cares about others, treats them with respect, and seeks to minimize their distress. Leslie has also found contentment, and does not suffer from anxiety, alienation, frustration, disappointment, or depression.

Perhaps you assume that all is well with Leslie, yet many philosophers believe that Leslie's life might not be worthwhile. Indeed, to use terms employed by Neera K. Badhwar, Leslie's life might be wasted, servile, pathetic, ignoble, and a failure.[1] How could such a negative assessment be justified?

Susan Wolf maintains that if Leslie is not actively engaged in projects of worth, then Leslie's life lacks meaning.[2] Richard Kraut asserts that Leslie is not healthy unless possessing, developing, and enjoying cognitive, affective, sensory, and social powers.[3] Stephen Darwall finds that Leslie's life lacks merit unless it focuses on things that matter, such as beauty and knowledge.[4] Neera K. Badhwar insists that Leslie's life is worthless if not possessing

---

1. Badhwar, *Well-Being*, 46, 72, 80, 84, 222.

2. Wolf, *Meaning in Life*, 9.

3. Kraut, *What is Good and Why*, 172.

4. Darwall, *Welfare and Rational Care*, 95.

wholeheartedness, i.e., "an integrated intellectual-emotional disposition to live autonomously."[5]

Such attacks on the value of other people's lives are seriously misguided. Would any of these philosophers, meeting Leslie, be willing to say, "I understand that others think well of you, but I'm sorry to say that your life lacks meaning." Furthermore, "if only you had studied, for example, epistemology, thus engaging in a project of worth, developing your cognitive powers, focusing on things that matter, and thinking more independently, your life would have been as meaningful as mine." Such arrogance would be intolerable.

Suppose Leslie is married with two children, works as a salesperson in a department store, sings in a chorus, golfs (with enthusiasm but little success), and struggles to solve the daily crossword puzzle. Would Leslie's life nevertheless be wasted because of a failure, as Badhwar says, "to seek truth or understanding about important aspects of [his or her] own life and human life in general"?[6]

Remember whose lives are dedicated to that goal—philosophers. No wonder they find the most value in their own endeavors.

I would urge, instead, that we acknowledge the dignity of others by recognizing people's worth regardless of whether their activity is primarily intellectual or manual, whether they prefer symphonies or gospel music, whether they choose solitude or the company of others, whether they are conformists or nonconformists, and whether they admire or are bored by philosophical inquiry.

So long as individuals act ethically, they are surely worthy. And if they find satisfaction, let us not say that they have failed. The only failure is our inability to appreciate the variety of good lives.

---

5. Badhwar, *Well-Being*, 112.

6. Badhwar, *Well-Being*, 23.

3

Choosing the Experience Machine

co-authored with Christine Vitrano

IN A FREQUENTLY CITED and widely admired thought experiment, Robert Nozick offers the following hypothetical:

> Suppose there were an experience machine that would give you any experience you desired. Super-duper neuropsychologists could stimulate your brain so that you would think and feel you were writing a great novel, or making a friend, or reading an interesting book. All the time you would be floating in a tank, with electrodes attached to your brain. Would you plug in?[1]

Nozick presumes that no one would choose this option, and presents three reasons. First, "we want to *do* certain things, and not just have the experience of doing them." Second, "we want to *be* a certain way, to be a certain sort of person." Third, "plugging in. . .limits us to a man-made reality." Nozick concludes that because we would not use an experience machine, "something matters to us in addition to experience."[2]

In the decades since Nozick posed this puzzle and presented his solution, virtually all philosophers have taken his treatment as

1. Nozick, *Anarchy, State, and Utopia*, 42–43.
2. Nozick, *Anarchy, State, and Utopia*, 43.

conclusive. Almost no one has argued that people would choose the experience machine.

To find such unanimity among philosophers is unexpected, but the situation is especially surprising because Nozick's conclusion appears mistaken. In support of this view, we shall offer various reasons why an individual might be inclined to choose the experience machine. We illustrate these by the use of examples as least as plausible as the experience machine itself.

I

First, consider cases in which people may not desire to *do* certain things but instead want to have the experience of doing them. For example, one of the pleasures of going to the movies is having the opportunity to experience adventures we would not risk undertaking in reality. While safe in our plush seats, we can feel the excitement of skiing precipitously down a steep mountain, participating in dangerous international intrigue, or battling a typhoon. Yet how many of us actually wish to *do* any of these things?[3] Such cases demonstrate that using an experience machine is not in principle objectionable. The only controversial issue is the length of time for which you would be willing to employ it.

The cinema, however, is not the only case in which we seek appearance rather than reality. Consider the popularity of bungee jumping, roller coasters, aggressive computer games, or reenactments of Civil War battles. All these activities offer participants

---

3. Jonathan Glover recognizes that the experience machine could be considered "an improved version of the cinema," and for that reason admits that he would try the machine "for brief periods" (Glover, *What Sorts of People*, 92). But after doubting that most people would choose to plug in for the rest of their lives (thus suggesting that some might make such a choice), he goes awry by arguing against plugging in being made compulsory, a suggestion neither Nozick nor anyone else has proposed. Thomas Hurka also recognizes that "we use TV and movies as substitute experience machines." Yet he maintains that "for many of us a whole life of good feeling would lack important human goods" (Hurka, *Best Things in Life*, 69). As for others who might not share his desire for hardships, he has no comment.

the experience of pursuing thrilling adventures without facing the real-life activities they simulate.

Another sort of escape from reality is offered by psychedelic drugs. Nozick notes that these are viewed by some "as mere local experience machines," but he does not draw the inference that their widespread use suggests that many would welcome the opportunity not only to drop out but also to plug in.[4] A similar point could be made about the widespread use of alcohol to distort reality.[5]

Granted, the examples we have discussed so far involve individuals who might use the machine only occasionally. And in a later discussion Nozick reformulates his challenge: "The question is not whether to try the machine temporarily, but whether to enter it for the rest of your life."[6]

In response, let us turn to cases in which people, to change who they are, might choose the experience machine for the rest of their lives. Consider golf enthusiasts who struggle to master this most intractable of games. Doing so at a professional level necessitates spending innumerable hours hitting thousands of golf balls day after day over a period of at least a decade. Not many of us would choose to spend our lives in such tiresome training (even if we had the needed ability to excel, as most of us do not). Suppose, however, that without any preparation you could experience hitting massive drives, pinpoint iron shots, and precision putts, all while hearing the roars of the crowd as you win major championships. Wouldn't many amateur golfers want that life? Wouldn't they be willing to trade their frustration on the fairways for a life of golfing triumphs?

Or consider the ardent music lover who dreams of becoming a concert violinist. Few persons, even if they had the necessary talent, would choose to exhaust their energy and patience in such

---

4. Nozick, *Anarchy, State, and Utopia*, 44.

5. Torbjorn Tannajo cites the use of drugs as the support for his contention that Nozick's argument is "in an almost obvious way unsound" (Tannajo, "Narrow Hedonism," 79–98). No other philosopher of whom we are aware has reached the same conclusion.

6. Nozick, *Examined Life*, 105.

a strenuous effort. Suppose, though, that without any exertion they could have the experience of performing recitals in great halls and appearing with the world's leading symphony orchestras, each time receiving adulation from a cheering audience. Might some not be willing to trade their lives to undergo such experiences?

Imagine that instead of living your own life, you could choose to live the life of Alexander the Great, Cleopatra, or Babe Ruth. Do you suppose no one willingly would make that trade, even though the experience machine could be programmed to omit a life's tribulations and focus on its triumphs? Or perhaps you prefer the cinematic adventures of Clark Gable, Katharine Hepburn, or Humphrey Bogart. Would no one choose their lives? How about living the life of secret agent James Bond? Wouldn't that option tempt some?

Another sort of case concerns individuals who would wish to change their characters. For example, how would you feel if you possessed the moral and intellectual virtues of the Buddha? The experience machine could provide the answer.

Or suppose you wish to have been present at the trial of Socrates, the Lincoln-Douglas debates, or the riot at the Paris premiere of Stravinsky's *Le Sacre du printemps*. The experience machine could make you a spectator at these events. Of course, you wouldn't actually be there. Your experience, however, would be indistinguishable from reality.

The experience machine would also enable you to have experiences of inestimable personal value. For example, you could experience a world inhabited by your loved ones who have died. In our dreams we often imagine such a scenario and, when awakened, are disappointed that the dream did not continue. Suppose, however, you could opt for the vision to endure. Wouldn't many do so?

Or imagine living again in the time and place of your younger days. Such is the plot of "Walking Distance," an early episode of *The Twilight Zone*, written by the program's creator, Rod Serling, with evocative music by the famed composer Bernard Hermann.[7] Con-

---

7. For an insightful assessment of the script, see Cahn, *Walking Distance*,

sidered by many the finest show of the entire series, this nostalgic story captures the poignant tale of world-weary advertising executive Martin Sloan, who returns to his home town, only to find it exactly as it was at the time of his youth. He confronts his parents, who believe he is a lunatic, and tries to converse with himself as a child, but the frightened boy runs away. Martin, however, cannot remain there. As his father, who at last understands the situation, insists, "only one summer to every customer." In a moving voice-over at the conclusion, Serling observes:

> Martin Sloan, age thirty-six, Vice president in charge of media. Successful in most things— but not in the one effort that all men try at some time in their lives—trying to go home again. And also like all men perhaps there'll be an occasion—maybe a summer night sometime—when he'll look up from what he's doing and listen to the distant music of a calliope— and hear the voices and the laughter of the people and the places of his past. And perhaps across his mind there'll flit a little errant wish— that a man might not have to become old— never outgrow the parks and the merry-go-rounds of his youth. And he'll smile then, too, because he'll know it is just an errant wish. Some wisp of memory not too important really. Some laughing ghosts that cross a man's mind.[8]

But the experience machine could fulfill that wish. Would no one choose to do so?

Another reason why individuals might choose the experience machine is a desire to escape a life of sorrow or even agony. Nozick, when revisiting the idea of the experience machine, declares such cases irrelevant, perhaps because he presumes that they occur infrequently.[9] The truth, however, is otherwise. The plight of so many unfortunate people is captured in this verse of William Blake:

> Every Night & every Morn
> Some to Misery are Born.

5–23.

8. Cahn, *Walking Distance*, 18–19.

9. Nozick, *Examined Life*, 105.

Every Morn & every Night
Some are Born to sweet delight.
Some are Born to sweet delight,
Some are Born to Endless Night.[10]

Those born in the latter circumstance would surely choose the delights of the experience machine in place of their dreadful lives on earth.

How many unfortunates are in this position? Consider Schopenhauer's view:

> Life with its hourly, daily, weekly, yearly, little, greater, and great misfortunes, with its deluded hopes and its accidents destroying all our calculations, bears so distinctly the impression of something with which we must become disgusted, that it is hard to conceive how one has been able to mistake this and allow oneself to be persuaded that life is there in order to be thankfully enjoyed, and that man exists in order to be happy.[11]

One need not be as pessimistic as Schopenhauer to sympathize with his outlook. If the experience machine offers joys in place of tortures of mind and body, the burden of argument would surely rest on those who would urge against its use. After all, we avoid the pain of surgery by the use of anesthesia; we thereby avoid reality. If one's life itself is little more than a succession of pains, why not opt for the delights of the experience machine?

Nozick asserts that "plugging into the machine is a kind of suicide."[12] He says, however, that the machine enables one to choose a "lifetime of bliss."[13] Hence wouldn't plugging in be the closest we could come to heaven on earth? After all, what is heaven supposed to be if not eternal bliss?

---

10. Blake, "Auguries of Innocence," 510.

11. Schopenhauer, "On the Variety and Suffering of Life," 115.

12. Nozick, *Anarchy, State, and Utopia*, 43.

13. Nozick, *Anarchy, State, and Utopia*, 43.

Nozick concludes that we desire to be "in contact with reality."[14] Knowing what we do of reality, though, why assume that remaining in touch with it is invariably preferable to a lifetime of bliss?

II

The array of cases we have presented demonstrates that the assumption that no one would use the experience machine is implausible. Indeed, were such a machine on the market, a wise investor would seek to purchase it, or at least buy stock in the company that manufactured it.

But what lessons are we supposed to learn from the claim that no one would choose the machine? Jonathan Glover believes Nozick's thought experiment demonstrates that "we care about more than our own experiences."[15] No doubt some of us do, and some don't. We shouldn't, however, confuse caring about something with being unwilling to trade it under appropriate circumstances. Epidural anesthesia is chosen by many women to ease the pain of labor and delivery, but doing so does not imply that they devalue the reality of childbirth. Similarly, choosing to plug into the experience machine does not imply a lack of concern for reality. Such concern may simply be overridden.

James Griffin presumes that rejecting the experience machine demonstrates that knowing the truth rather than being comforted by delusions makes for "a better life."[16] That conclusion is easier to reach, however, if one's life is satisfying. But for those suffering in "endless night," the value of delusions should not be so quickly dismissed. In any case, would you want to know the truth regarding the time and circumstances of your death? Indeed, grasping more of the truth does not always lead to a better life. Who would want

---

14. Nozick, *Anarchy, State, and Utopia*, 45.

15. Glover, *What Sorts of People*, 285.

16. Griffin, *Well-Being*, 9.

to discern the deepest thoughts of all others? The truth matters, but it may be traded for something more valuable.

We don't doubt that some people would prefer reality to the experience machine. Does that supposition imply, as L. W. Sumner claims, that "being in touch with reality makes for a better life"?[17] That conclusion doesn't follow unless we assume that following one's preferences always leads to a better life. Yet while some of our choices are wise, others are not. Whether we choose to plug into the experience machine does not prove the good sense of doing so.

Nozick believes that we value reality over the mere experience of it. As our cases demonstrate, however, sometimes we don't value reality highly or even at all. As Hume in his *Dialogues Concerning Nature Religion* puts the point in the mouth of the orthodox believer Demea:

> The whole earth. . .is cursed and polluted. A perpetual war is kindled amongst all living creatures. Necessity, hunger, want stimulate the strong and courageous; fear, anxiety, terror agitate the weak and infirm. The first entrance into life gives anguish to the new-born infant and to its wretched parent; weakness, impotence, distress attend each stage of that life, and it is, at last, finished in agony and horror.[18]

Such is reality, and for good reason some would wish to explore other possibilities. They may still value aspects of reality but would be willing to trade them for something they believe more valuable. Whether such exchanges would be wise depends on the circumstances. To suppose, however, that regardless of the attractiveness of the alternatives such a choice would never be made, is unwarranted. Once that error is recognized, Nozick's experience machine can be seen as what it is: a dream for which many may yearn, but not evidence that mere experience is insufficient for happiness.

17. Sumner, *Welfare, Happiness, and Ethics*, 96

18. Hume, *Dialogues Concerning Natural Religion*, pt. 10, par. 8.

PART II

RELIGIOUS BELIEF

4

THE THEODICY TRAP

THE WORLD IS BESET by evils. Could it, therefore, have been created by an omnipotent, omni-benevolent God? Epicurus thought not, and put the point succinctly: Is God willing to prevent evil, but not able? Then He is impotent. Is He able, but not willing? Then He is malevolent. Is He both able and willing? From where, therefore, comes evil?

This line of argument is commonly known as "the problem of evil," and developing a solution is the goal of theodicy, a term derived from the Greek words *theos* and *dike*, meaning "God" and "righteous." If a theodicy works, then it demonstrates at least that a world containing evil could have been the creation of an omnipotent, omni-benevolent God. But is that situation merely an unlikely possibility, or a probability? The most successful theodicy would show that the world's widespread evils should have been expected, given that the creator was all-powerful and all-good.

A theodicy is shaky if it explains only some evils but not all. For if certain evils are inconsistent with the existence of God, then their occurrence would disprove God's existence. Yet as experience makes all too clear, if an evil is possible, then it likely has occurred or will occur. Thus a successful theodicy needs to offer a justification for all possible evils. Only then is theism secure.

Suppose, for example, an earthquake occurs, killing thousands. Some might suppose that such an event would undermine belief in an all-powerful, all-good creator of the world. With a successful theodicy in hand, however, theism would be safe from refutation by such an event; its occurrence could be explained without limiting the power or goodness of God.

No wonder, then, that theists have long sought a successful theodicy. Were this goal attained, however, it would lead into a trap. For if God's existence were compatible with all evils, why should belief in God afford any comfort?

For example, Psalm 23 refers to God as our shepherd. Even as "I walk through a valley of deepest darkness, I fear no harm, for You are with me."[1] But why shouldn't I fear harms? They may befall me even if I am in God's care.

So Job learns, when he suffers grievously despite having not sinned. He was being watched over by God, but to no avail. Granted, in the end he is rewarded, but his ten dead children are not so fortunate. Yet they, too, presumably were being watched over by God.

Perhaps comfort is supposed to be found eventually in a next world, although that obscure concept is not a central theme in the Hebrew Scriptures. As to this world, however, not only can good things happen to bad people, and bad things happen to good people, but the most wonderful things may happen to the worst people, and the most awful things may happen to the best people. A successful theodicy envisions and justifies all these possibilities.

That the world was designed by an omnipotent, omni-benevolent God might appear to be a basis for optimism. A successful theodicy, however, proves that God's plan could include every horrible occurrence imaginable, thus destroying any reason to be hopeful about events in this world.

Consider an analogous case. Suppose I recommend a restaurant, praising it for the excellence of its management. During your visit, though, you find the ambience gloomy, the service poor, the food unpalatable, and the cost high. When you express

1. Pss 23:4.

disappointment about your visit, I present an argument proving that all these conditions are consistent with the management's excellence. Indeed, I even show that such conditions are to be expected in a restaurant with excellent management. You may not know how to refute my argument, but the next time I recommend a restaurant on the basis of its excellent management, you won't be eager to eat there. After all, my argument that an excellent management is consistent with an inferior dining experience implies that you have no reason to suppose that conditions at a restaurant with an excellent management will be in any way satisfactory.

Similarly, if God's plan for the world is consistent with a succession of the worst evils, you have no reason to suppose that conditions in the world need ever be in any way satisfactory. A drought, for example, might persist for years, while a successful theodicy would provide a justification for the continuing oppressive condition. Moreover, praying to God for rain in those circumstances appears to make little sense, for if the draught is justified, why should God stop it?

To highlight this problem, consider the well-known theodicy offered by Richard Swinburne.[2] He assures us that God's plans require "much evil." Moral evils, those that human beings inflict on one another, are necessary for free will. Hence my suffering as a result of your freely chosen evil action is not entirely a loss for me, because I have contributed to the cause of freedom. "Those who are allowed to die for their country and thereby save their country from foreign oppression are privileged." Thus according to this theodicy, being the victim of injustice has a good side, even for the victim.

As for natural evils, those for which human beings are not responsible, Swinburne maintains that they give us the opportunity to perform worthy acts. Pain, for instance, helps develop patience. Therefore injustice contributes to the good not only as a by-product of free choice but also as an effective means for victims to develop moral virtue.

---

2. Swinburne, *Is There a God?*, 96, 102, 113.

Swinburne's theodicy is so powerful that it implies not only that our world would be worse without evils but that heaven would be better if it contained them. In fact, Swinburne doesn't hesitate to draw this conclusion. He notes that heaven "lacks a few goods which our world contains, including the good of being able to reject the good."

No wonder that, in reflecting on his theodicy, Swinburne warns: "I would not in most cases recommend that a pastor give this chapter to victims of sudden distress at their worst moment, to read for consolation. But this is not because its arguments are unsound; it is simply that most people in deep despair need comfort, not argument."

Swinburne recognizes that his theodicy offers no comfort. The crucial point, however, is that no successful theodicy does; it justifies whatever events occur.

The sad fate of some is to suffer through years filled with sorrow and suffering, anguish and agony, even tortures of mind and body. A successful theodicy, however, would demonstrate that such wretched lives, no matter how common, do not conflict with belief in an omnipotent, omni-benevolent God. If they did, then theism would fall prey to the problem of evil. A successful theodicy would solve that problem but leave believers without any reason to expect support from God.

In that connection, recall the moving words of the Levite benediction:

> The Lord bless you and protect you!
> The Lord deal kindly and graciously with you!
> The Lord bestow His favor upon you and grant you peace![3]

A successful theodicy would prove that even with the Lord's blessing and protection, the Lord's kindness and graciousness, and the Lord's favor, your life on earth may be filled with evils, and you shouldn't expect God to alleviate them. After all, a successful theology has demonstrated that whatever evils occur, God views them as contributing to a greater good.

3. Num 6:24–26.

If this conclusion is unacceptable to theists, one way out would be to cease searching for a successful theodicy, instead continuing to conceive God as omni-benevolent but recognizing God's power as limited. In that case, faced with a pandemic, for instance, theists could perhaps find some comfort in the realization that God wished to provide immediate relief but was unable to do so. Moreover, praying to God would still be appropriate, although God could not grant every request.

Admittedly this account of God's nature would likely appeal to few theists. By accepting it, however, they would escape having to accept the implausible claim made by every successful theodicy that God considers all evils, including all pandemics, to be enhancements of life.

5

Why Worship God?

We bow the head in reverence, and worship the King of kings, the
Holy One, praised be He.

—*THE UNION PRAYER BOOK FOR JEWISH WORSHIP*

LET US ASSUME THAT the universe was created and is sustained
by God, an omnipotent, omniscient, omni-benevolent Being. My
question is: what attitude should we take toward God? Should we
praise God? Should we bow the head in reverence? Should we
worship God?

If, like the Psalmist, you believe that "The Heavens declare
the glory of God, the sky proclaims His handiwork,"[1] then praising God presents no problem. Of course, some, like the author of
the Book of Ecclesiastes, have been little impressed by our world,
saying, "Then I accounted those who died long ago more fortunate
than those who are still living; and happier than either are those
who have not yet come into being and have never witnessed the
miseries that go on under the sun."[2] Although the goodness of creation is thus open to dispute, praising God presents no conceptual
difficulties.

1. Ps 19:2.
2. Eccl 4:2.

32

How about displaying reverence for God? To revere someone is to regard that individual with profound respect. Thus you might revere your mother or father, a beloved teacher, an inspiring political leader, or a great artist. In that sense, you might also revere God, indeed, more than any other being.

Would bowing the head be an appropriate way to display reverence? The answer is not clear. In Japan, bowing is a means to offer thanks, show respect, or express an apology. Intended for such purposes, bowing the head or bending the knee is unproblematic. But what if bowing is intended as a form of worship, denigrating oneself and exalting another beyond challenge? Is worshipping in that sense ever appropriate?

To seek an answer, let us consider a hypothetical case. Suppose a fabulously wealthy developer decides to create a utopian town, providing all its inhabitants with a spacious home, a generous bank account, and the finest in schools, parks, roads, stores, and a variety of other amenities. Let us suppose further that this developer is a person of extraordinary wisdom and kindness, who has planned to maintain the town far into the future. Presuming you are an inhabitant of the town, what should be your attitude toward the developer?

No doubt you would admire the developer's planning and appreciate the developer's generosity. Probably you would support the town's expressing its gratitude to the developer by placing a statue in the town square, naming a building, or celebrating an annual holiday. Which option would be most appropriate would to a large extent depend on what the developer prefers. As it happens, however, the developer answers no questions and is unavailable to anyone seeking direct interaction. Thus none can be sure what the developer wishes.

How about worshipping the developer? Would that response make sense? Few, if any, would think so. But why the reluctance? After all, the developer has created and sustained the town, holds power over the town, has displayed extraordinary knowledge in planning the town, and acts as benevolently as possible toward the town's inhabitants. Why, then, would the town's inhabitants hesitate to worship the developer?

An obvious reply is that the developer is not God. But how significant are the differences between them?

First consider their powers. God is far more powerful than the developer, but the developer appears to possess all the power the town requires. Granted, the developer doesn't decide matters of life and death, but had the developer chosen to become the town's despot, judging who is to live and who to die, would exercising those powers render the developer more admirable? Quite the opposite, most would suppose. Furthermore, would the developer become worthier of worship by creating more utopian towns? Hardly.

Another difference between the developer and God relates to the scope of their respective knowledge. God knows everything that can be known, while the developer doesn't, but the developer has near total knowledge of the town. If the developer acquired knowledge about more places, more people, and more things, would that increase in knowledge render the developer worthy of worship? Again, no. Suppose the developer was a master psychologist who understood the desires and fears of each person in the town. Would that knowledge increase the appropriateness of worshipping the developer? Hardly. After all, while the finest performers in a field of endeavor may deserve honors, even a perfect performance doesn't call for worshipping the performer.

The developer always acts ethically toward the town's inhabitants, while God always acts rightly in every situation. But does quantity of right acts matter? Most of us act rightly sometimes, some act rightly most times, and a few act rightly at all times. But even if the developer is in the latter category, worshipping the developer still appears inappropriate. Indeed, were an individual to seek to be an object of worship, that desire would itself suggest weakness, not strength, of character. Why would that same principle not apply to God? In that regard, recall the words attributed to God by the prophet Amos:

I loathe, I spurn your festivals,

I am not appeased by your solemn assemblies,

If you offer Me burnt offerings—or your meal offerings—

I will not accept them;

I will pay no heed

To your gifts of fatlings,

Spare Me the sound of your hymns,

And let Me not hear the music of your lutes,

But let justice well up like waters,

Righteousness like an unfailing stream.[3]

Which of God's attributes, if any, is supposed to imply that God seeks or deserves worship? God's power is overwhelming, but power alone does not call for worship. God's knowledge is as complete as possible, but immense learning, while admirable, does not imply the appropriateness of worship. God's goodness is perfect, but to be good is to be made uncomfortable by praise. God created and sustained the universe, but the developer's having created and sustained the town (or innumerable such towns) does not suggest that the developer should be worshipped. Why is God different? Granted, while each attribute of God taken alone does not justify the worship of God, perhaps all together do. I see no argument, however, why possessing any combination of attributes renders God worthier of worship than does each attribute separately.

What, then, should be the appropriate attitude toward God? The best answer I know is implicit in chapter 18 of the Book of Genesis, in which God tells Abraham that God is considering destroying the cities of Sodom and Gomorrah. Here is the key passage:

> Abraham came forward and said, "Will you sweep away the innocent along with the guilty? What if there should be fifty innocent within the city, will You then wipe out the place and not forgive it for the sake of the innocent who are in it? Far be it from You to do such a thing, to bring death upon the innocent as well as the guilty, so

3. Amos 5:21–24.

that innocent and guilty fare alike. Far be it from You! Shall not the Judge of all the earth deal justly?" And the Lord answered, "If I find within the city of Sodom fifty innocent ones, I will forgive the whole place for their sake. Abraham spoke up, saying, "Here I venture to speak to my Lord, I who am but dust and ashes: What if the fifty innocent should lack five? Will You destroy the whole city for want of the five?" And He answered, "I will not destroy if I find forty-five there." But he spoke to Him again, and said, "What if forty should be found there?" And He answered, "I will not do it, for the sake of the forty." And he said, "Let not my Lord be angry if I go on: What if thirty should be found there?" And He answered, "I will not do it if I find thirty there." And he said, "I venture again to speak to my Lord: What if twenty should be found there?" And He answered, "I will not destroy, for the sake of the twenty." And he said, "Let not my Lord be angry if I speak but this last time. What if ten should be found there?" And He answered, "I will not destroy, for the sake of the ten."[4]

While the story four chapters later, of God's commanding Abraham to prepare the sacrifice of his son Isaac, has attracted far more attention than the story of Abraham bargaining with God, I find the earlier story more revelatory about the appropriate relationship between human beings and God.

To begin with, Abraham recognizes his own cosmic insignificance as compared to God. Nevertheless, Abraham challenges the justice of God's plan to destroy Sodom. Hence the story is inconsistent with the divine command theory of morality, according to which justice is defined by whatever God commands. Abraham asks God to reflect on the justice of destroying Sodom, should the city contains fifty innocent inhabitants. If the goodness of an action were determined by God's will, then God's plan to destroy Sodom could not be shown to be wrong, for whatever God commanded would be right. By appealing to God's wish to act justly, however, Abraham convinces God to alter the plan, because God's original

4. Gen 18:23–32.

proposal is not just. But then the concept of justice is not merely a matter of God's will but an independent standard that God recognizes. If the supposed reason to worship God is that God's will creates morality, then that consideration does not serve as a justification for worshipping God, because although God always acts in accordance with morality, God does not create morality.

Note that, while Abraham recognizes that his powers are no match for God's, God is subject to the power of reason. Abraham could not have prevented God from destroying Sodom, but the power inherent in sound reasoning is decisive, and Abraham is using that power to change the will of God. Thus humanity is not without leverage against God, and if the basis for worshipping God is supposed to be that God has all power and humanity has none, the story of Abraham's bargaining with God indicates that such a justification is mistaken.

Notice that God is subject to change. God begins by planning to destroy Sodom, but then agrees to condition that decision on whether the city might contain innocent people, whether fifty, forty-five, forty, thirty, twenty, or ten. For those who worship God because God is thought to be unchanging, that rationale is ineffective, because God keeps changing the number of innocent persons required to save Sodom from destruction.

Still, God might be thought worthy of worship because of God's controlling whether we live or die. In the chilling words of the Puritan minister and philosopher Jonathan Edwards:

> The God that holds you over the pit of Hell, much as one holds a spider, or some loathsome insect, over the fire, abhors you, and is dreadfully provoked; his wrath towards you burns like fire; he looks upon you as worthy of nothing else, but to be cast into the fire; he is of purer eyes than to bear to have you in his sight; you are ten thousand times so abominable in his eyes as the most hateful venomous serpent is in ours. You have offended him infinitely more than ever a stubborn rebel did his prince; and yet 'tis nothing but his hand that holds you from falling into that fire every moment.

No wonder Edwards was unable to finish his sermon as "there was a great moaning and crying out throughout the whole house. . . . The tumult only increased as the 'shrieks and cries were piercing and amazing."[5] In short, Edwards forced the congregation to confront the awful truth that they were doomed, and only God could save them.

Surely God as described by Edwards is terrifying. The lesson is this: make a wrong move with God, and you will be condemned to a horrendous fate. No wonder religious services often call for bowing one's head, averting one's eyes, kneeling, and even groveling. In the spirit of humbling oneself, rituals are performed and prayers recited as exactly as possible, so that God is not angered. The prevalent emotion is fear, along with the hope that we and our loved ones will be spared God's wrath.

The obvious analogy is between God and a despot. In the despot's country, inhabitants take great pains to avoid engaging in any actions that would call attention to themselves and attract the despot's wrath. Obviously, however, no despot should be worshiped, although inhabitants may be forced to go through the motions of appearing to worship the despot.

Of course, the despot, unlike God, is hardly benevolent and surely not omni-benevolent. The goodness of God, however, is not a reason to worship God but, on the contrary, a reason *not* to worship God, because a good being would not want to be worshiped. And that insight is exemplified in the story of Abraham bargaining with God about the destruction of Sodom.

When Abraham suggests to God that God needs to think further about the action God is about to take, God does not disregard Abraham, berate him, or tell him that he has no right to be raising doubts. Rather, God listens to Abraham's reasoning and makes a suitable adjustment to the plan as originally proposed. Had Abraham worshiped God, then Abraham would simply have accepted God's plan, praising it and extolling God. To worship is to venerate or pay homage, not to question and challenge.

---

5. The quoted material is found in Marsden, *Jonathan Edwards*, 220, 223.

The eminent rabbi Mordecai M. Kaplan, founder of Reconstructionist Judaism, which explicitly rejects supernaturalism, was once a guest speaker at a religious service where the congregation recited the proverb "Trust in the Lord with all thy heart and lean not upon thine own understanding."[6] Rabbi Kaplan announced to the assemblage that these words were ones he refused to utter, because he could not relinquish the right to trust his own powers of reason. His attitude is an echo of Abraham's bargaining with God, for Abraham did not trust God's judgment about Sodom. Instead, Abraham relied on his own understanding and successfully challenged God's plan.

Those who believe in God should follow the example of Abraham, praising God as frequently and fervently as wished, acclaiming God's omnipotence, omniscience, and omni-benevolence, and thanking God profusely for creating and sustaining the universe. Like Abraham, though, believers should not treat the word of God as beyond challenge by human reason. God may be worthy of as much praise and gratitude as human beings can offer, but even God is not to be worshipped.

6. Prov 3:5.

6

HEAVEN

ACCORDING TO A POPULAR evangelical hymn, "I'm on my way to Heaven, and the journey gets sweeter every day." The music is compelling, but we might wonder: Where is Heaven, how long until we arrive, who are the inhabitants, what activities occur there, and why, as the song says, does our desire to go increase every day?

For many theists, the importance of believing in God rests on the possibility of a blissful afterlife. After all, if God exists but Heaven does not, how important would God's existence be? Granted, if God exists, then theists are correct in their metaphysical belief, but why would being right about that matter be more important than holding a correct view about any other metaphysical claim, such as whether time flows or mathematical entities are real? In other words, why do so many display deep concern whether God exists?

A popular answer is that if God exists, those who live morally will be rewarded with an afterlife in which they abide forever in a place of joy. In short, they will spend eternity in Heaven.

Yet that notion raises numerous difficulties. To begin, where is Heaven? Those who speak of Heaven often look upward, but would travel to Mars, Jupiter, or the nearest galaxy bring us closer to Heaven? Or is Heaven not in space? Might it have no location? Yet if people go to Heaven, they go somewhere. But to where do they journey, how long does the trip take, and what might they experience on the way? No one knows.

When we die, our bodies stop functioning and may even be destroyed. What form will they take in Heaven? Will they look as they did when we were ten, forty, or seventy? If a person suffered from diabetes, will the resurrected body suffer from the disease? Indeed, if a person was ill for decades, will the resurrected body suddenly enjoy health that was rarely, if ever, attained in life? No one knows.

If a new body is provided, would the resurrected person be identical to the person who died? If a ship is destroyed and an identical one built, the second is different from the first. Similarly, if a person is destroyed and an identical one created, the second is different from the first. In that case, the original person would be lost.

A way to avoid difficulties about resurrected bodies is to suppose that after death what survives are not bodies but souls. Yet what is a soul? Supposedly, when added to a body, a soul converts that body into a person. Of course, if the soul itself can think and feel, it is a person without a body. How, then, does it become a person when it enters a body? Can two souls inhabit a single body, or is the arrangement only one soul per person? Do non-human animals have souls? How would we know?

A crucial question concerns the personality of the resurrected person. Suppose Smith is charitable, loyal, and humorous, and enjoys gardening, listening to classical music, playing golf, and taking trips with friends. After death, will the resurrected Smith have the same character and interests? If not, in what sense is the resurrected person appropriately identified as Smith?

To see an even greater difficulty, consider two acquaintances, Peters and Peterson. Peters looks forward to spending eternity with Peterson, whereas Peterson looks forward to being forever free of Peters. Assuming they retain their fundamental likes and dislikes, how can they both attain heavenly bliss?

Other problems arise when we try to understand the relationship between those in Heaven and those on Earth. The common supposition is that those who die maintain an interest in events of this world. For example, a loving father who taught his daughter to become a championship swimmer will presumably, after his death, take pride if his daughter wins an Olympic medal. But that supposition, while perhaps comforting to the daughter, turns those in Heaven into spectators of the living, watching intently as events unfold. What, then, becomes of heavenly bliss? How can Heaven bring peaceful existence if the triumphs and tragedies of this world remain the focus of attention?

If those in Heaven are unconcerned about events on Earth, however, the relationship between those alive and those dead is broken. After all, if the father of the swimming champion no longer cares whether his daughter succeeds, athletically or otherwise, in what sense is he still her loving father?

As we age, we watch members of succeeding generations take our places. Thus our attention may turn increasingly away from the events of this world and focus increasingly on contemplating the next. Such is the reason why, in the words of the evangelical hymn, the journey to Heaven grows sweeter every day.

Yet the question remains: what will we find in Heaven? Consider the case of Willie Mays, the spectacular baseball player whose greatest joy was to play the game he loved. What does Heaven offer him? Presumably bats, balls, and gloves are not found there, so what does Willie Mays do? Assuming he is the same person who made that spectacular catch in the 1954 World Series, how can the pleasures that supposedly await him in Heaven match those he knew on Earth?

One answer is that worldly delights pale in comparison with the delights of experiencing God. But how long can we find ecstasy in sheer contemplation, even if the object of our attention is divine? In the absence of events, even the most passionate love grows dull. Eventually we want to do something with or for those we love, not just remain endlessly in their presence.

If those in Heaven have no worldly interests and talents, then they have lost their individuality. Yet if such differences are maintained, why assume they will all find the same delight in the presence of the divine?

For instance, if someone who was cantankerous in life goes to Heaven, does that person remain cantankerous? If so, what becomes of eternal bliss? If not, what becomes of the individual's distinctive characteristics?

Even granted these innumerable difficulties, the hope for Heaven is understandable. After all, death looms for all. Like boaters riding long rapids, flowing inexorably toward a deadly waterfall, we can take pleasure in the passing scene so long as we do not focus on where we are headed. What we cannot do, however, is stop the current or change its direction. We are caught in the grip of time. Yet Heaven offers us an escape. There we can live forever, surrounded by those for whom we care, and safe in the eternal home, abiding in the light and goodness of God.

The vision is compelling, even if unreasonable. Yet philosophical reflection never forces us to any conclusion. Every argument requires premises, and if the conclusion of an argument is found unacceptable, the premises can be denied.

In this case, the vision of Heaven may be so attractive that many may wish to believe in the idea regardless of any arguments against it. They may consider all questions of who, what, where, why, and how to be mere quibbles.

Furthermore, even false beliefs can play a positive role in our lives. Suppose, for example, that as a youngster you were told by your parents that your uncle left the country decades ago and now lives in an inaccessible region of the world. He is an upright man who cares for you deeply and has high hopes for you. He also possesses sizable resources and in mysterious ways keeps track of your activities.

As you grow up, your belief in your uncle plays a crucial role in your life. When your hopes are stymied or your confidence wanes, you find renewed strength in the thought that your uncle loves you and wants you to succeed. In short, your belief in your uncle enables you to deal with life's problems and achieve important goals.

If, however, you have been misled and your supposed uncle never existed, would you be better off learning the truth? Perhaps not.

Analogously, suppose that as a youngster you were told by your parents that your uncle died decades ago but still watches over you from Heaven. Let us assume that this belief plays a crucial role in your life, enabling you to deal with life's problems and achieve important goals.

If Heaven does not exist, would you be better off learning the truth? Again, perhaps not.

Still, we need to remember that the desire to reach Heaven may lead some individuals to commit horrendous crimes and thereby seek to secure a glorious future in the next world. That result, too, may be a consequence of disregarding the canons of reason.

In conclusion, we may wonder whether the concept of Heaven, regardless of its rational justification, does more good or ill. To that question, though, philosophy alone cannot provide any definitive answer.

PART III

ACADEMIC LIFE

7

FACULTY APPOINTMENTS

SEARCHING FOR A NEW colleague is rarely a smooth process. Indeed, it can intensify departmental friction or create it where none existed.

Once a department is informed that it can make an appointment, the announcement of the position needs to be developed. The question then arises as to which subfields, if any, will be given prominence in the search. Ideally, the decision should reflect fair assessment of the department's needs. Too often, however, that criterion is ignored.

Imagine a music department that has four members teaching the history of Western music. Let us designate them as *A*, *B*, *C*, and *D*. *A* teaches Renaissance music; *B* specializes in the baroque age, particularly J. S. Bach; *C* focuses on the classical period, especially Beethoven; and *D* teaches music of the twentieth and twenty-first centuries. What is missing?

A neutral observer would immediately recognize a crucial gap: composers of the romantic era, including Brahms and Wagner.

That area, however, may *not* be the department's first priority. Consider how the discussion might proceed:

A: I'm supposed to cover all of Renaissance music, but I focus on the early period. We need someone for the middle and late.

B: While my work is centered on Bach, there's so much more in the baroque. Let's add someone who can handle it. The nineteenth century is important, but I haven't heard much call from students for Tchaikovsky.

C: Recently I've been concentrating on Beethoven's quartets. How about someone who can delve into Haydn and Mozart? We can also use someone who could teach the yearlong survey in the history of music.

D: Contemporary music is so varied that we need another person to do it justice. I have a friend from graduate school who works in electronic music and would be a terrific colleague.

The pattern is clear. Every member hopes to use the appointment to advance personal interests.

Here is commentary to help explain the discussion.

A, the historian of the Renaissance, seeks a colleague with similar interests so as to have someone at hand for discussion and assistance. Rather than saying so, however, *A* stresses differences between the early and later Renaissance, then argues that the department needs a specialist in both. The problem, of course, is that any subject can be divided into smaller units and the argument made that each unit needs coverage. We might term this strategy "divide and augment."

Suppose, for instance, instead of one professor doing Shakespeare, we split the field into tragedies, histories, comedies, and romances, then argue for specialists in each area. And how about someone to cover Shakespeare's sonnets? Suddenly five professors are teaching Shakespeare. In a large department, multiple scholars for a single area might be reasonable, but this small program has room for only one historian of Renaissance music.

B, the historian of baroque music, also uses the "divide and augment" strategy, followed by an appeal to lack of student interest in nineteenth-century music. But why expect students to urge that a subject they have never studied should be taught? If baroque music were not in the curriculum, would students complain?

C, the scholar of the classical period, wants to focus on Beethoven and also seeks someone to teach the history of music survey that requires extensive preparation and covers materials outside any one instructor's interests. C proposes that the members of the department avoid that demanding assignment by giving it to a newcomer.

D, the contemporary music scholar, uses the "divide and augment" strategy, then adds what might be labeled the "I have a friend" approach. This maneuver typically leads a professor to overrate pals, then become angry if colleagues do not share this inflated view. To avoid the problem, all department members should agree that in considering candidates, no one is under any obligation to be favorably disposed toward anyone else's friend. All subsequent discussion of candidates should be untarnished by personal attachments, and anyone suggesting a friend should stay out of discussion of that candidate. Failure to do so is one of the most common reasons for unfortunate appointments.

Once the members of the department present their opinions, the discussion usually turns repetitive and possibly rather unpleasant, as each one reiterates ever more forcefully already-stated positions. In accord with academic manners, however, attacks are never launched against the value of anyone else's research area but instead framed as defenses of one's own. How to break the impasse?

One solution calls for the advertisement to include a list of specializations sought: the middle and late Renaissance, the baroque age, Haydn and Mozart, the nineteenth century, and electronic music. That approach will likely satisfy the four members but appear strange to potential candidates who will wonder why the department has such an unusual collection of priorities.

Here an effective dean might step in and insist that the complex advertisement be sharpened. Such a request, although sensible, is why faculty often consider administrators to be obstacles.

How might the department react to the dean's objection? A common move is to declare that the search will seek the best person, regardless of field. This step might temporarily satisfy all involved, but down the road produce poor results.

The reason is revelatory. While specialists have some acquaintance with other subject matters, only regarding their own are they familiar with a broad spectrum of faculty members, programs, and scholarly activities. Therefore, unless one candidate is clearly superior to all others (an infrequent situation), each professor will find "the best" to be the best in that specialist's field and try to forge a majority in favor of that candidate. As the infighting continues, the field most likely to be neglected is the one currently unrepresented; it is least known by the members, yet most in need of an appointment. In the end, however, whichever professor is politically savvy and most determined carries the day. If, after a year or two, another opening appears and again the same area is disregarded, the department will become lopsided, perhaps for decades.

Why did this situation develop? Because the dean allowed the department to advertise the position as open. What should have happened is that when the compromise was proposed, the dean should have responded, "No one's working in the nineteenth century. Unless that's the specialty you announce, the search is over." The department would be upset but would likely bow to the dean in order to make an appointment.

Eventually, if the dean monitors the search process carefully, the department will settle on a candidate who can cover the romantic period. As a result, the students will benefit and have the opportunity to study the music of Mendelssohn, Chopin, and Verdi, among so many other favorites. Even the faculty may eventually appreciate the perspective of their new colleague and realize the wisdom of offering broader coverage.

In any case, discord is likely to accompany the process. Indeed, if for nefarious reasons someone wanted to create turmoil in an amiable department, I cannot think of a more effective strategy than offering the members an opportunity to undertake a search. Even if they do not reach consensus, the members should consider themselves fortunate if their good relations survive.

8

ACADEMIC VOTING

HERE'S A COMMON SITUATION. A department plans to choose six candidates to be interviewed for one opening. At the meeting where the vote is to occur, the suggestion is made that each member of the department be given three votes, and the six candidates receiving the most votes will be invited.

Suppose the department has ten members, of whom nine prefer candidate A to all others, then candidate B, then candidate C, and on down to candidate Z. One member of the department, however, prefers the candidates in the reverse order, rating candidate Z the highest, Y the next highest, and on down to candidate A, who is rated the lowest.

Now the voting takes place. Nine members vote for candidates A, B, and C. The other member votes for Z, Y, and X. So A, B, and C each receive nine votes, and the next highest candidates are Z, Y, and X, each receiving one vote. So A, B, C, Z, Y, and X are invited for interviews.

The problem, of course, is that almost every member of the department hasn't the slightest interest in Z, Y, and X, preferring D, E, F, and every other candidate to Z, Y, and X. Yet Z, Y, and X have been invited. What has gone wrong?

The procedure has violated an essential principle of fair voting. Each voter must be given the same number of votes as the number of candidates to be selected. Thus in this case each department member should have been given six votes, because six applicants were to be chosen. Using that principle would have resulted in invitations to *A, B, C, D, E,* and *F,* who were preferred by the overwhelming majority of the department. *Z, Y,* and *X* were the candidates least preferred by almost all members of the department and should not have been invited.

Keep in mind, then, that when a department votes to choose a certain number of people for any purpose, voters need to be given the same number of votes as the number of people to be selected. In that way voting will be fair and accurately reflect the will of the majority.

When you vote for judges on Election Day, you are entitled to cast the same number of votes as the number of judges to be selected. The same principle applies in academic voting.

9

THE AMBIGUITIES OF AFFIRMATIVE ACTION

"DO YOU BELIEVE IN affirmative action?" Any simple answer to this familiar question is misguided, because the question itself is extraordinarily ambiguous. My major aim in this essay is to show why.

First, the term "affirmative action" refers to two entirely different policies. One is taking appropriate steps to eradicate practices of racial, gender, religious, or ethnic discrimination. Such *procedural affirmative action*, as I call it, is intended to ensure that applicants for positions are judged on their merits, not their identities. Steps to insure procedural affirmative action include open announcements of opportunities, blind reviewing, and a variety of efforts to eliminate from decision procedures any policies that harbor prejudice, however vestigial.

In another sense of "affirmative action," which I call *preferential* affirma*tive action*, the term signifies making special efforts to recruit individuals who meet institutional goals related, for example, to racial, gender, or ethnic identity. Doing so calls for attending to the same criteria that procedural affirmative action deems irrelevant. While procedural affirmative action is uncontroversial, preferential affirmative action is not, and in the remainder of this discussion my use of the term "affirmative action" should be understood as referring to "preferential affirmative action."

What is the point of affirmative action? Is it to offset past discrimination, counteract present unfairness, or achieve future equality? The first is often referred to as "compensation," the second as "a level playing field," and the third "diversity."

Note that each of these aims can be defended independently of the others. Compensation for past wrongs may be owed, although at present the playing field is level and future diversity is not sought. Or the playing field at present may not be level, although compensation for past wrongs is not owed and future diversity is not sought. Or future diversity may be sought, although compensation for past wrongs is not owed and presently the playing field is level.

Of course, all three factors might be relevant, but each requires a different justification and calls for a different remedy. For example, past wrongs would be offset if suitable compensation were made, but once provided to the appropriate recipients, no other steps would be needed. Present wrongs would be corrected if actions were taken that would level the playing field, but doing so would be consistent with unequal outcomes. Future equality would require continuing attention to ensure that an appropriate balance, once achieved, would never be lost. Thus defenders of affirmative action would favor at least one of these policies but not necessarily more than one.

Regarding the frequently-cited appeal to diversity, the concept itself, if unmodified, is vacuous. Consider, for example, a sample of the innumerable respects in which people can differ: age, religion, nationality, regional background, economic resources, military experience, bodily appearance, physical soundness, sexual orientation, marital status, ethical standards, political commitments, or cultural values. The crucial question is: which sorts of diversity should be sought?

Imagine a ten-person philosophy department which has no African American, no woman, no non-American, no person under fifty, no non-Christian, no registered Republican, none whose doctoral degree is from other than an Ivy League University, none who served in a war, none who is homosexual, none who was ever on welfare, none who is physically challenged, none whose work is outside the analytic tradition, none who specializes in aesthetics, and none who is widely heralded for success as a teacher. When the next appointment is made, which characteristics should be stressed so as to render this department more diverse? I know of no compelling answer.

To put the matter vividly, suppose that the candidates for a position in that department include an African American, a woman, an Argentinian, a thirty-year-old, a Buddhist, a Republican, someone whose doctoral degree is from Indiana University, a veteran, someone who was once on welfare, someone who uses a wheelchair, a homosexual, a specialist in continental philosophy, an aesthetician, and a widely acclaimed teacher. Which one should be favored purely on grounds of enhancing diversity? The question is unanswerable.

Suppose the suggestion is made that the sorts of diversity to be sought are those of groups that have suffered discrimination. The problem with this approach is clearly put by John Kekes:

> It is true that American blacks, Native Americans, Hispanics, and women have suffered injustices as a group. But so have homosexuals, epileptics, the urban and the rural poor, the physically ugly, those whose careers were ruined by McCarthyism, prostitutes, the obese, and so forth. . . .
>
> There have been some attempts to deny that there is an analogy between these two classes of victims. It has been said that the first were unjustly discriminated against due to racial or sexual prejudice and that this is not true of the second. This is indeed so. But why should we accept the suggestion. . .that the only form of injustice relevant to preferential treatment is that which is due to racial or sexual prejudice? Injustice occurs in many forms, and those who value justice will surely object to all of them.[1]

Kekes' reasoning is cogent. In addition, another difficulty looms for the proposal to seek diversity only of groups that have

---

1. Kekes, "Injustice of Strong Affirmative Action," 151.

suffered discrimination. Consider, for instance, a department in which most of the faculty are women. In certain fields, for example, nursing, dental hygiene, and elementary education, such departments are common. If diversity by gender is of value, then such a department, when making its next appointment, should prefer a man. Yet men as a group have not been victims of discrimination. On the other hand, Jews and Asians have been victims of discrimination but do not presently suffer from minimal representation. Thus the question of which groups need enhancement to achieve diversity cannot be answered satisfactorily by an appeal to history.

Nor is the situation clarified by arguing that the appeal to diversity favors members of a group who experience the world from a distinctive standpoint. Celia Wolf-Devine has aptly described this claim as a form of "stereotyping" that is "demeaning." As she puts it, "A Hispanic who is a Republican is no less a Hispanic, and a woman who is not a feminist is no less a woman."[2] Furthermore, are Hispanic men and women supposed to have the same point of view in virtue of their common ethnicity, or are they supposed to have different points of view in virtue of their different genders? And why suppose that a person's point of view is determined only by race, gender, or ethnicity? Why not also by the numerous other significant respects in which people differ, such as age, religion, sexual orientation, political outlook, and so on?

Every affirmative action plan calls for giving preference to members of certain groups, but the concept of preference itself is unclear. For example, imagine a search for an assistant professor in which one hundred persons apply, and among them are some who are members of a group designated for affirmative action. Let us refer to those individuals as *AA* candidates.

Suppose the dean has permitted five applicants to be invited for campus interviews. After studying one hundred dossiers, the department ranks ten candidates as outstanding, twenty as good, fifty as merely qualified, and twenty as unqualified. Let us suppose that four applicants are *AA* candidates, and among them one is

---

2. Wolf-Devine, "Proportional Representation," 230.

ranked as outstanding, one as good, one as merely qualified, and one as unqualified.

The key question is: Given that *AA* candidates are to be preferred, what forms of preference are called for? One possibility is to interview any *AA* candidate who is outstanding, regardless of the merits of any other outstanding candidates. Another possibility is to interview any *AA* candidate who is good, even though many other candidates are stronger. Yet another possibility is to interview any *AA* candidate who is qualified, even though again most candidates are stronger. A theoretical possibility is to interview even unqualified *AA* candidates, although I know of no one who would support that policy, so let us set it aside. What remains are three different models of preference, any of which might be defended.

Next assume two *AA* candidates are chosen for interviews, one who was ranked as outstanding and another ranked as good. Afterwards, the department places the outstanding candidate second and the other fifth. Does giving preference to *AA* candidates require that the second candidate be offered the position? And if the candidate ranked second receives a more attractive offer and withdraws from consideration, need the candidate now ranked fifth be preferred?

Of course, an *AA* candidate may be ranked the highest, thus avoiding any problems. Otherwise the call for giving preference requires an interpretation that is rarely, if ever, announced beforehand.

Suppose, for instance, that the administration has told the department that its next appointment needs to be an *AA* candidate. Shouldn't that information be publicized, so that those who are members of the groups in question and those who are not can plan accordingly? Surely those who have instituted a policy of preference believe that their action is within moral and legal bounds. No one should object, therefore, to stating that policy without equivocation. Yet the usual approach is to keep such information under wraps.

Such secrecy, however, leads to difficulties. For instance, during my years as an administrator I once met with a candidate who was considering our school's offer of a faculty position and sought my assurance that he would have been chosen regardless of affirmative action. I responded truthfully that he was held in high regard but that I didn't know the answer to his concern. Yet I believe he was entitled to raise the matter, for whatever the steps required by a school's affirmative action policy, surely they should not be hidden.

Thus far my examples have all been drawn from cases of faculty appointments, but different considerations may arise in justifying affirmative action in student admissions. After all, colleges traditionally take account of a high school applicant's athletic prowess, community service, personal relationships to alumni, and geographic home. Such criteria, however, are not considered in a faculty search. No wonder defenders of affirmative action are most comfortable supporting it in the context of a complex admissions decision involving many non-academic factors, while opponents most often think of the policy in relation to assessing the research and teaching of applicants for faculty positions. The two decisions are different in kind, and the same arguments may not apply to both.

In addition, circumstances matter. Consider a department that has never appointed a woman and, when given a promising opportunity, refuses even to interview one. Suppose the dean insists that in the next search process some women should be interviewed, and if a woman with a superlative record is found, she should be appointed. Would opponents of affirmative action object? I think not.

On the other hand, consider a department that announces its intention to achieve a goal of fifty percent women, and in its next search prefers a minimally qualified woman to a man who is widely regarded as far more promising as a researcher, teacher, and contributor to the life of the department. If the dean insists that the man be appointed, would proponents of affirmative action be upset? Again, I think not.

Both these cases are admittedly extreme, although not entirely unrealistic, but the lesson is that presuming affirmative action to be at odds with merit, as its opponents do, or to be a means of obtaining justice, as its defenders do, are oversimplifications. The context matters.

Returning now to the question with which I began, "Do you believe in affirmative action," any answer depends on whether procedural or preferential affirmative action is under discussion; whether the goal is compensation, a level playing field, or diversity; what sorts of diversity are sought; what sorts of preference are proposed; whether the policy will be made public; whether the focus is faculty appointments or student admissions; and whether any special circumstances are part of the context. This information is needed to give a sensible answer to the original question or even appreciate its complexities.

PART IV

DOCTORAL EDUCATION

10

ORIENTATION

FOR MANY YEARS I attended my department's opening week orientation for new doctoral students. While most arrived unsure or even apprehensive, all were eager to understand more fully the situation they faced. Few faculty participated, however, and those that did treated the occasion lightly, engaging in banter with one another and evincing little concern for the anxieties of the beginners.

Over time the pattern of these meetings was unchanged. The chair began by inviting the newcomers to introduce themselves and indicate their specialty. Those who replied with uncertainty received patronizing smiles, while the response that invariably caused derisive laughter was, "I plan to teach."

Subsequently the faculty were asked to describe their current scholarly work. The newcomers listened attentively, nodding as if comprehending every word while struggling to understand any of what was said.

Next, the students were invited to ask about the program, but being unfamiliar with it, did not have much to contribute. The message they received, however, was clear and emphatic: find an area of research and publish as much as possible. Although nearly all the doctoral students were eventually expected to teach undergraduates, not a word was said about this responsibility. Nor was any advice given about how best to survive the hoops and hurdles of doctoral study. Instead, the session typically concluded early, when the chair announced that the essentials had been covered and that the time had come for wine and cheese.

Perhaps this approach to orientation is unique to my program. Yet I presume other departments engage in similar practices. I would suggest, however, that we can do better. Here are ten pieces of advice that should prove useful to those heading into the thickets of academia.

1. Read widely. As a college student, you were only responsible for works the instructor assigned, but as a scholar you create your own reading lists. The more literature you master, the less reliant you are on faculty.

2. Write frequently. Putting one's ideas into written form aids precise thinking. If you doubt the effectiveness of your style, consult an appropriate handbook.[1]

3. Don't delay. Do not allow lack of confidence to lead you to put off fulfilling requirements, taking examinations, or submitting papers. The longer you wait, the more the pressure mounts. Postponement is not progress.

4. Meet the professors. Eventually you will need to choose an advisor to guide your dissertation. Whether by attending a lecture, conversing at a departmental function, or visiting during office hours, seek a professor whose interests, methodology, and personality are in sync with your own.

5. Meet other students. They can offer helpful advice about courses, professors, and strategies. Furthermore, discussion with colleagues is one of the pleasures of the profession. Granted, solitude may stimulate creativity, but scholars do not flourish in isolation. Rather, they rely on publishers, librarians, and one another.

6. Meet professional colleagues. Those at other institutions who share your interests can offer valuable contacts. You can

1. See, for example, Cahn and Cahn, *Polishing Your Prose.*

encounter such individuals at scholarly conferences, whether you merely attend or, better yet, serve as a speaker, commentator, or session chair. By the way, volunteers are often sought for these positions. Furthermore, because almost all the attendees will be active scholars in your field, they will be as eager to meet you as you are to meet them.

7. Seek a dissertation topic. As you proceed, be alert for a potential project that engages your interest, is of appropriate scope, and is innovative without being idiosyncratic. Choosing your subject wisely is a crucial step toward finishing your work in a reasonable time and maximizing your chances for a desirable academic position. Publishing along the way is a plus, but finding a winning dissertation topic is invaluable.

8. Diversify your interests. You don't want to be a one-trick pony, a scholar with only one area of expertise who offers endless variations on the same theme. At an interview, you may well be asked about your interests apart from your dissertation. You should have a couple you can discuss.

9. Plan to teach. Before long you will be expected to assume the obligations and challenges of teaching undergraduates. Not all your students will have an immediate attraction to your subject. Thus, as you proceed, consider how you might motivate students to explore central issues in your discipline.[2]

10. Maintain your dignity. Unfortunately, graduate professors occasionally take advantage of students in various ways, including destructive criticism, inordinate delays in returning work, inaccessibility, or mixing professional with personal concerns. Even worse, professors have had more than their share of scandals involving forms of sexual harassment or abuse. In all these instances students should not abide mistreatment but immediately report any incidents to the appropriate administrator, whether the department chair or a dean.

2. For some specific suggestions, see Cahn, *Teaching Philosophy*.

Thereafter inaction from the authorities should be met with forceful protest.

An orientation meeting that explained these points might take a couple of hours but would be worth attending, even in the absence of refreshments. Furthermore, the session would emphasize to all that the primary aim of doctoral education is not to enhance faculty interests or prerogatives but to support students in their efforts to succeed as scholars and teachers.

11

The Basics

Many years ago, when my late friend James Rachels and I were assistant professors at New York University, we used to discuss all aspects of departmental life. Among our musings was the speculation that our colleagues vastly overestimated how much graduate students knew about philosophical literature. Therefore, as an experiment, we drew up a list of fifty famous books, most in the history of philosophy but a few in contemporary philosophy, and asked our students to name the authors. The results confirmed our fears. The highest score any student achieved was in the thirties, most couldn't identify even half the books, and a few knew barely ten. Meanwhile, our colleagues proceeded as if the students were highly knowledgeable.

I believe that those responsible for doctoral education continue to overestimate how much graduate students know about basic philosophical texts and issues. That assumption is comfortable, because it absolves the faculty from ensuring that students possess fundamental information about the field.

Let me pose a few questions for consideration:

1. When your department awards a student a doctoral degree, do you believe that the student should be able to explain such fundamental matters as the differences between rationalist

and empiricist theories of knowledge, materialist and dualist theories of mind, and deontological and consequentialist theories of ethics?

2. When your department awards a student a doctoral degree, do you believe that the student should have familiarity with writings of such towering figures as Plato, Aristotle, Descartes, Hobbes, Hume, and Kant?

3. Assuming the answers to (1) and (2) are "yes," does your department require core courses or comprehensive examinations to ensure that students possess such knowledge?

4. If not, are you concerned about recommending for faculty positions those who have mastered a specialty but nevertheless lack essential knowledge about the most crucial philosophical issues and the most influential philosophical thinkers?

5. If your department does not have required core courses or comprehensive examinations, do you at least provide students with annotated reading lists to guide them in acquiring fundamental knowledge?

In the absence of such safeguards, students are apt to reveal their ignorance at unfortunate times, including classroom presentations, dissertation defenses, interviews, and professional lectures. For example, I once taught a doctoral course in which a well-regarded graduate student offered a brief talk defending the compatibility of freedom and determinism. He indicated that he had embraced this position only after reading a recent journal article defending the view. When I asked whether he was familiar with anyone in the history of philosophy who had supported compatibilism, he expressed surprise that the position was not newly discovered. When I referred him to Hume's arguments, the student responded that he was unfamiliar with them. In fact, he admitted that had never read anything by Hume.

I was not entirely surprised because years before, our department, seeking to become more professionally competitive, had eliminated all core courses and replaced comprehensive examinations with research papers. This student was a victim of those changes.

Thus I urge departments to ask themselves: Do we have in place a system that would save students from falling prey to such a lack of essential information?

12

THE HIDDEN CURRICULUM

THE TERM "HIDDEN CURRICULUM" refers to the unstated attitudes that are often communicated to students as a by-product of school life. While the phrase is usually employed in the context of elementary and secondary education, it also applies at the graduate level, where future professors are acculturated to careers in academia.

One implicit message is that prestige follows from accomplishment as a researcher, not as a teacher. For example, which candidate for a faculty position is usually viewed as more attractive, the promising researcher or the promising teacher? Which of the two is more likely to be judged a strong candidate for tenure? The answers and the lesson are obvious: excellence in research is judged as far more important than excellence in teaching.

A second message is that faculty members are entitled to put their own interests ahead of those of their students. Consider how departments decide graduate course offerings. The procedure is for individual professors to announce the topics of their choice; then that conglomeration becomes the curriculum. The list may be unbalanced or of little use to those preparing for their careers, but such concerns are apt to be viewed as irrelevant. The focus is not on meeting student needs but on satisfying faculty desires.

Similarly, in a course ostensibly devoted to a survey of a major field of philosophy, the instructor may decide to distribute chapters of the instructor's own forthcoming book and ask students to help edit the manuscript. Whether this procedure is the best way to promote understanding of the fundamentals of the announced field is not even an issue.

Another instance of professorial primacy is readers who take months to return a chapter of a dissertation, explaining the delay by pointing to publishing deadlines they themselves face. Apparently the student's deadlines for finishing the dissertation and obtaining a faculty position are not as important.

A third message is that when you listen to a speaker, you should pretend you understand what is being said, even when you don't. How many times do faculty members and students sit through a presentation grasping little or nothing of it, yet unwilling to say so? Instead, they nod as if comprehending every word. In short, contra Socrates, the goal is always to appear knowledgeable.

But just the opposite is the case. Professors should encourage students in class to indicate whenever they become confused. And such admissions should be met not with a put-down but with a compliment for intellectual honesty. After all, those afraid to admit what they do not grasp are defenseless against others who indulge in obfuscation.

These days signs around the country tell us that if we see something, we should say something. Graduate students should be advised to follow an analogous rule: If you don't understand something, say something.

Professors should be aware of the subliminal messages sent to graduate students, who learn from the hidden curriculum and eventually pass it on. Thus are unfortunate attitudes and practices transferred from one generation to another.

PART V

PUZZLES

13

THE AFFIRMATIVE ACTION PUZZLE

Suppose your department has no faculty members from a particular racial, ethnic, or sexual group. In the past some have applied, but none has ever been chosen. A representative of your school's Board of Trustees consults you about a proposal, currently being considered by the Board, to fund a professorship for your department that is open only to scholars from that particular racial, ethnic, or sexual group. Would you support this idea? If so, would you agree that the announcement of the position should inform potential applicants of its special feature, so that all can decide whether to apply in light of full information about the search?

This situation was addressed in an essay by Tom L. Beauchamp, who wrote:

> Incompleteness in advertising sometimes stems from fear of legal liability but more often from fear of departmental embarrassment and harm either to reputation or to future recruiting efforts. The greater moral embarrassment, however, is that we academics fear making public what we believe to be morally commendable and mandatory in our recruiting efforts. There is something deeply

wrong in this circumstance, one that virtually every academic department now faces.[1]

But what, if anything, is wrong? Is it the proposed practice, the law, the lack of moral courage on the part of faculty, or something else?

1. Beauchamp, "Quotas by Any Name," 215.

14

THE BUS PUZZLE

HERE'S A REAL-LIFE MORAL problem based on my own experience in New York City.

Two men boarded a bus, sat down, and saw under their seats a package of gloves that appeared to have been newly purchased. After some discussion, one man indicated that he intended to keep the gloves for himself. An older fellow across the aisle, listening to the conversation, told the two that they should give the gloves to the bus driver, who would take them to the lost-and-found. This older man further explained that whoever had paid for the gloves would want them returned. Indeed, he claimed that taking the gloves under those circumstances would be stealing. In response, the two men insisted that they still intended to keep the gloves.

Moments later, the older man rose to leave. As he passed the two others, he grabbed the package, gave the gloves to the driver, and hurried off.

What the bus driver did with the package I do not know. Perhaps he gave the gloves to the lost-and-found, contributed them to a relief organization, or returned them to the first two men. He might even have kept them for himself.

Whatever the outcome, given these circumstances, how should we morally assess the behavior of the two men who found the package, as well as the words and actions of the older man and the possible plans of the bus driver?

15

THE ALTRUISM PUZZLE

I

Suppose I uncover a plot to set off a bomb that would destroy a city. Only I am in position to foil the scheme. Doing so, however, would cost me my life. I may choose, of course, to sacrifice myself and thereby save thousands of others. But am I morally obligated to do so?

II

The altruism puzzle suggests a quandary that is worth attention. If in the case described I have a moral obligation to sacrifice my life, then in another situation I might be morally obligated to relinquish my property, my physical well-being, or my pursuit of happiness. After all, if when my life is at risk, I cannot choose self-interest over altruism, how can I do so to preserve something of lesser value than my life? Granted, in other situations the consequences of my choices might not be so calamitous, but considering the vast amount of suffering in our world, I could be obligated to abandon, if not my life, at least all my personal interests, devoting myself exclusively to providing much-needed aid to others. I would become, in the words of the subtitle of *The Pirates of Penzance*, "The Slave of Duty."

On the other hand, if in the case described I do not have a moral obligation to sacrifice my life because that price would be too great, why should I ever be morally obligated to give up my property, my physical well-being, or my pursuit of happiness? Admittedly, such values are not as precious to me as my life, but still I may find surrendering them excessively costly. If I do, why can't I again choose self-interest over morality? Furthermore, wouldn't the justification for my doing so be even stronger in ordinary circumstances, where the consequences of my acting solely for my own advantage are far less horrific?

In sum, the altruism puzzle calls for accepting one alternative and dealing with the consequences. But which option is the one to choose?

PART VI

REMINISCENCES

16

THE ROAD TRAVELED

CAREERS USUALLY REFLECT CHANCE as well as choice. Mine has been no exception.

I

In 1959, after graduating from Woodmere Academy (now Lawrence Woodmere Academy), where most memorably I studied Latin for a year with the celebrated poet and translator Rolfe Humphries, I entered Columbia College. I registered as pre-law but still lacked a career goal. Two years later, as yet unsure of my vocation and seeking further understanding of the legal profession, I enrolled in a course titled "Philosophy of Law." I did not realize that the professor, Ernest Nagel, was an internationally renowned philosopher of science, but I became enamored of his brilliance, erudition, and modest demeanor. He spoke so clearly and answered questions so patiently that I was inspired to try to emulate him, and thus I began to consider pursuing the study of philosophy. While taking a second course of his devoted to epistemology, I ventured into his office and inquired whether he thought I might become a philosopher. His response was encouraging, and consequently my tentative plan to attend law school was shelved.

II

Wishing to stay in New York, I applied and was accepted at Columbia's Graduate Department of Philosophy. I soon realized, however, that I needed a specialty and was not sure which to select. I did not have sufficient background in science to choose Professor Nagel's area. I had an interest in history, particularly American history, but no special concern for the philosophy of history. I had performed extensively as a pianist and organist, but preferred playing music to discussing it. I had knowledge of Judaism, but the philosophy department offered no courses in philosophy of religion.

Hence when I went to register for the first time, I chose haphazardly, selecting a class in American philosophy and another in the religion department. Then I asked the adviser if he had any suggestions. He recommended "Philosophical Analysis," a course to be taught by Professor Richard Taylor, who had just arrived from Brown University. I knew nothing about him and had no idea what was meant by "philosophical analysis," but in the absence of promising alternatives, I enrolled. Little did I know that my life was about to change.

Professor Taylor's teaching style, which he called "the blackboard and chalk method," was a revelation. The approach didn't require mastery of either the history of philosophy or current journal literature. Rather, he wrote on the board the steps of an argument, and students were supposed to decide if the reasoning was sound.

The task appeared straightforward, yet offering an answer that could withstand criticism proved difficult. Nevertheless, I welcomed this challenge, because it depended not on extensive research but only on hard thinking.

The first topic for discussion was a proof for fatalism. I didn't realize the argument was Professor Taylor's own but submitted a paper defending it against criticisms he had suggested we consider. When a couple of days later he returned my essay, I was stunned by his laudatory comments. Indeed, he urged me to prepare the piece for publication and use it as a chapter of my dissertation. Suddenly my life had focus: I knew my specialty, my adviser, and my calling.

From then on I attended every graduate class Professor Taylor taught and was a regular visitor to his office. Eventually, as he had predicted, the paper was published and served as a chapter of my dissertation. But as I finished writing my thesis, Professor Taylor left Columbia to join the faculty at the University of Rochester, and under the generous sponsorship of Professor Arthur Danto I completed my work.

Nevertheless I stayed in touch with Professor Taylor, who kindly returned to New York to attend my dissertation defense. Indeed, for a few summers I visited him at his home in Trumansburg, New York, just outside of Ithaca. There he kept his beehives, for, as I discovered, he was world renowned as an apiarist and wrote a column for the leading beekeeping journal. In fact, as he told me, he was better known among beekeepers than among philosophers.

III

The time had now come for me to seek a faculty position. Appointments then were far easier to obtain than they became a few years later, and one fall morning the secretary in the Philosophy Department inquired if I would like to be interviewed for a position the next year at Vassar College. I hesitated because I had not anticipated a post at a women's college (only later did Vassar become co-ed), but fortunately the secretary scheduled an interview, conducted by the long-time chair of the Vassar department, Vernon Venable. In those days openings were not publicly announced, and Professor Venable's search procedure consisted of visiting potential candidates only at Harvard, Yale, and Columbia.

During our brief meeting he inquired whether I was a Wittgensteinian. Although not entirely sure of his meaning, I replied that I wasn't. That answer turned out to be helpful, because, as Professor Venable subsequently explained, he didn't care for the work of Wittgenstein.

Afterwards he asked me to examine the Vassar catalogue and indicate which philosophy courses I would prefer to teach, which I would be willing to teach, and which I would not want to teach. That task was not difficult until I came to a course titled "Philosophy of Education." I had not heard of this subject and wondered into which category I should place it. I reasoned fallaciously that because I was interested in philosophy and in education (having taught religious studies to grade school students), I would also be interested in philosophy of education. Therefore I listed it among the subjects I would prefer to teach.

Little did I realize that expressing enthusiasm for that course would be a primary reason I would be chosen for the position. In fact, the department was required to offer the course every semester to meet the needs of the education students, and no member of the philosophy faculty or any other applicants wanted to accept the assignment. Ironically, the field became a specialty of mine, and soon after leaving Vassar, having taught the course four times, I edited my own anthology, which in a second edition still remains in use.

Before I began at Vassar, though, I had a free semester, and Professor Taylor recommended me to the faculty at Dartmouth College, where someone was needed for one semester to teach discussion sections of their introductory course. I gratefully accepted an offer, and spent a delightful term in Hanover, New Hampshire, where I heard captivating lectures to the two hundred assembled students by instructors Willis Doney, Timothy Duggan, and Bernard Gert. All three welcomed me, and as a beginner I was grateful for their cordiality.

The department sponsored colloquia, and I still remember the visit by the well-known historian of philosophy Father Frederick Copleston. After his talk he spent the rest of the evening answering with remarkable ease complex questions posed by faculty members seeking his assistance in handling especially challenging interpretative problems in the history of philosophy. Copleston's mastery was astounding.

IV

When fall came, I arrived at Vassar, and the two years I spent there proved to be among the happiest of my academic career. The students were first-rate and enthusiastic, while the faculty was knowledgeable and collegial. Indeed, I developed a special relationship with three members of the department.

One was John O'Connor, who later became executive director of the American Philosophical Association. John had earned his PhD at Harvard, while serving as a teaching assistant for both Quine and Rawls. John was an amazingly sharp thinker, yet easy to talk to. I learned much from our many conversations and enjoyed evenings in his company.

Another valued colleague was Garrett Vander Veer, who earned his degree at Yale, where he had been a student of the eminent idealist philosopher Brand Blanshard. While Garry and I had different philosophical backgrounds, I admired his academic integrity, the unwillingness to compromise reasonable standards. He was also a superb tennis player and skilled golfer, an unusual combination.

A third philosopher of note was Frank Tillman, to whom I had been introduced when we both attended the philosophical discussion group that met at Richard Taylor's apartment during his years at Columbia. After I had been at Vassar for a few weeks, Frank invited me to his large office. There he showed me heaps of material that he hoped to shape into a reader in aesthetics to be published by Harper & Row, for whom he served as a consultant. He asked if I might help him complete the volume and become its coeditor. I had no experience with such work but was pleased to participate. Eventually the book became my first anthology, introducing me to the world of publishing and resulting in my lifelong interest in such projects.

V

Although I enjoyed the ambiance at Vassar, I had always hoped to return to New York City; hence I was delighted when I received an invitation from Sidney Hook to join the faculty at New York University's Washington Square College in Greenwich Village.

The next five years, 1968–1973, were a time of disruption to our country and NYU, but for me they were a period of growth and excitement. I taught large undergraduate courses, sometimes with as many as a hundred or more students, took on graduate seminars with talented future scholars, some of whom would become nationally known, and accepted departmental and college-wide administrative positions. Chief among these was serving as head of the school's Educational Policy Committee, which was responsible for approving every department's proposed curricular changes. My responsibilities led me to meet many of the College's leading faculty members, an opportunity I relished.

Within the Department, I welcomed working with Professor Hook, whose writings I greatly admired. While he was a fierce debater concerning the issues of the day, he was always generous to students and colleagues. Although the mailboxes of the other members of the department were virtually empty, his was invariably stuffed with correspondence from around the world. I still recall entering his classroom to inform him that he had just received a telephone call from the White House. Yet his celebrity mattered no more to him than teaching a class or providing a letter of recommendation. I remain grateful for his many kindnesses.

Almost every day I ate lunch with my colleague James Rachels. In New York City, most faculty members do not spend much time at school but treat the entire city as a campus. Jim and I, however, were regularly in our offices, and, as we were about the same age and at the same stage of our careers, we conversed endlessly about philosophy, academic life, and our colleagues. He was remarkably affable, easy-going, and straightforward. The trait most foreign to him was pomposity. Typical was his reply to someone who asked about "films he had attended": "I don't attend films," he replied. "I go to movies."

Unfortunately, after we had been at NYU for several years, the school suffered a financial crisis, and the administrators, seeking to reduce the size of the faculty, urged that any faculty members able to leave should do so. Jim decided to accept an offer from the University of Miami, and when he departed, I was willing to consider other possibilities.

VI

An unusual one appeared at the University of Vermont, which advertised for a department chair. When the head of their search committee, psychologist George Albee, unexpectedly came to New York to visit me, I learned of a surprising situation. Only a few years before, the department was part of a single philosophy and religion department, and had only few members. When the university rapidly increased in size, the department did as well. Unfortunately, the process was handled without regard for appropriate academic procedures. The result was a large but undistinguished group of faculty, which considered itself estranged from the contemporary philosophical scene. Soon the department was at loggerheads with the administration, and Professor Albee was asked to head an ad hoc committee to find a new chair who could help to upgrade the department. He wondered if I might be willing to accept the assignment.

Had the situation at NYU been settled, I am sure I would have turned him down. But the challenge of building a strong department was appealing, and with some naïveté I decided to pursue the opportunity. When eventually an offer was made, I accepted.

The task, however, proved far more difficult than I had imagined. The Dean had invited me without the support of the department (which had opposed every outside candidate) and, with a couple of exceptions, the members did not want to be evaluated by usual academic standards. Most of the department's faculty, however, were untenured and subject to annual reappointment. After speaking with each of them at length and assessing their records, I recommended that four not be asked to return.

The matter became a cause célèbre. Yet after several months of turmoil the administration backed my recommendation. Three of the four were not reappointed, and the fourth was warned that unless he soon obtained his long-sought doctoral degree, he would not be continued; the following year he voluntarily departed.

Thus the department needed at least three new faculty members, and I had the primary responsibility for choosing them. The advertisement I placed resulted in the receipt of more than 700 applications. I studied each, then by myself interviewed the strongest candidates at the American Philosophical Association's Eastern Division meeting, and invited the most promising to campus.

Eventually, after persuading the Dean to allow four appointments, I chose Patricia Kitcher, Philip Kitcher, William Mann, and George Sher. I doubt if ever in my life I made a wiser academic decision. While their philosophical interests varied widely, all were first-rate teachers and future leading researchers who would eventually hold chairs in philosophy. But at the time I met them, their total publication record consisted of a single essay. (Since then they have written more than 25 books and 300 articles.)

All my new colleagues were extraordinarily conscientious and committed to work tirelessly to build the department, locally and nationally. The task was arduous, but the effort succeeded, and the University of Vermont gained a reputation for excellence in philosophy that remains to this day. Indeed, any list of the strongest undergraduate philosophy departments in the United States invariably includes the University of Vermont.

We knew our every step was open to criticism, so we proceeded as thoughtfully as possible. One of the first issues we faced was the need to select a departmental secretary. One applicant, Leslie Weiger, was the Dean's wife, and, although she was highly qualified, we wondered if choosing her would be wise. I saw no reason not to, because, as I told the others, we intended to do everything by the book, and we might as well ensure that the Dean was aware of our efforts. The choice was quickly justified, as our department received funding from the Dean's office for previously hard-to-obtain furniture and equipment, and over the decades our secretary was widely considered the best in the business.

We conducted subsequent searches with the utmost care, and our appointments were so strong that over time at least eight members of the department went on to professorships in leading doctoral programs. Given that for forty years thousands of undergraduates at the University of Vermont have had the opportunity to study philosophy with the guidance of an outstanding faculty, I consider the rebuilding of that department, however onerous, to be a major accomplishment.

VII

One afternoon early in 1978 I was sitting in my office looking through mail, when I came upon a letter from the Exxon Education Foundation. At first glance I thought it merely corporate advertising and almost discarded it. But looking more closely, I found an invitation, sent to many, to apply for a two-year term as a program officer at the Foundation. I knew nothing about foundations, but because this one was located in New York City, where I had been planning to spend an upcoming sabbatical year, I decided to apply, although I suspected that the odds I would be chosen were small.

I had heard nothing for months and had forgotten about the matter when I received a call inviting me for an interview. There the President of the Foundation, Robert L. Payton, who had been President of both Adelphi College and Hofstra University, asked one question that seemed especially important to him: Do you have an interest in high school education? I replied that I did, and to my surprise shortly thereafter I was offered the position, which I accepted. I suppose Bob Payton had intended to embark on a project dealing with secondary schools; therefore, he sought to appoint someone who would welcome the opportunity to participate. Strangely, however, no such program was ever developed, and the matter was never again mentioned.

When I began my work that summer at Exxon's headquarters, then on Sixth Avenue, I was given little guidance in how I should spend my time. I was asked to review several projects, but the criteria of evaluation were not explained. Furthermore, I found myself uncomfortable in corporate surroundings.

My only hope was that while I had been chosen to oversee humanities grants, I was told that someone else would be arriving to assess social science grants. As I waited, the time passed slowly, but when the new colleague appeared, my world was altered. His name was Leon Bramson, he had been a professor in the Department of Social Relations at Harvard and most recently was the founding chair of the Department of Sociology and Anthropology at Swarthmore College. Most important, he understood foundations and knew exactly how we should be handling our responsibilities. We bonded immediately, and he explained the opportunities we had as program officers to shape the Foundation's activity. Because the Exxon Corporation generously supported its Foundation, we had sufficient funds to take full advantage of our positions. We made innumerable contacts in the academic and foundation worlds and, with Bob Payton's support, developed a host of projects. They had nothing to do with the commercial aims of Exxon, but we had been asked by the Corporation to promote academic excellence, and we set out to do so.

Our terms were limited to two years; then we were expected to return to our schools. Lee, however, accepted an executive position at Exxon, providing social analysis of the impact of the company's business activities, while I was asked by the Rockefeller Foundation to become a program officer specializing in the humanities. The advantages for me were that I could stay in New York and further enhance my experience in the foundation world; the disadvantage was that, while continuing to be associated with the University of Vermont, I would no longer hold a tenured position. Taking a chance, I accepted the invitation and moved six blocks south on Sixth Avenue from the Exxon Education Foundation to the Rockefeller Foundation.

There I eventually was asked to become Acting Director for Humanities and worked with two rising stars in academic life: Steven D. Lavine, who would soon become the longtime President of the California Institute of the Arts; and Kathleen D. McCarthy, a noted historian and widely admired authority on foundations who would in time found a leading international Center on Philanthropy. Working with them both was a treat, and our efforts were greatly enhanced by the efficiency and creativity of our colleague Lynn Szwaja, one of the first women to graduate from Yale College, who would eventually serve for many years as program director for theology at the Henry Luce Foundation.

VIII

Yet after another year I began to miss academia and thought about returning. Before I could do so, however, a call came from the National Endowment for the Humanities in Washington, DC, inquiring if I would be interested in a position as the first Director of General Programs, a newly created area of the Endowment that would bring together all its support for public programs, such as museum exhibits and television shows.

In my foundation work I had become aware of the NEH but knew little about its operations. Nevertheless, the opportunity to work for the government in support of the humanities appealed to me, and I decided to accept the offer. Thus I moved to the nation's capital, taking up residence at the Watergate apartments (an elegant residence, despite the name's association with political scandal), and becoming a frequent visitor at the nearby Kennedy Center for the Performing Arts.

I supposed that given my experience in both a private and corporate foundation I would not find work in a government foundation to be vastly different, but the pressures were much greater and the pace frenetic. When the people's money is being spent, accountability is demanded, and the public is entitled to question each step in any decision process.

This point was brought home to me early on, when at a meeting of my 40-person staff, someone referred to the practice of providing "why not" letters. I was unfamiliar with that term and asked its meaning. I was told that any applicant who had been denied a grant could inquire why the proposal was turned down, and the staff was required to provide a detailed letter explaining the decision. In response I remarked that the only sort of letter with which I was familiar in my previous foundation work was a "that's it" letter: decisions were final, and no reasons given. In Washington, the staff was also expected to assist applicants in submitting materials for evaluation; where I had come from, those seeking grants were fortunate if anyone was willing to talk with them.

Admittedly, from the outside the government appears to work especially slowly, but inside the time passes with astonishing rapidity as program officers try to keep up with never-ending cycles of providing preparatory assistance, sorting thousands of applications, arranging peer evaluation, and making defensible decisions for eventual judgment by the Endowment's hierarchy. And if a request arrives from a member of Congress demanding an explanation of why a constituent's proposal was rejected, alarm bells ring throughout the agency while an answer is prepared as expeditiously as possible.

Shortly after arriving at the NEH, I realized I needed a veteran to help me through the process, and my one request to the administration was that I be given an experienced deputy. I interviewed several people for the position, but when I wasn't entirely comfortable with any of them and asked to meet others, I was told that one excellent person, George F. Farr, Jr., wasn't available, because he was too valuable to the division in which he worked. For that very reason he sounded appealing, and I argued strongly for the opportunity to interview him. When I did, I knew immediately that he was my choice, and as he was willing to join me, I convinced the reluctant administration to arrange his transfer.

Later I discovered that during my years at Vassar College, George had been a member of its English Department, but although I sensed I might have seen him around campus, we had never met. Without him, however, I could not have remained afloat in the turbulent waters at the NEH. As kind as he was knowledgeable and imaginative, he led me through the intricate processes, anticipating problems and ensuring we had adequate responses. Although he was formally my deputy, actually he was my guide.

One privilege I had was recommending personnel for any openings in my Division, and I took an opportunity to entice Leon Bramson from the Exxon Corporation to head a subunit at the NEH. He greatly enjoyed the work and stayed there for the remainder of his career.

The staff at the NEH was first-rate, but the difficulty at a government agency is dealing with the upper echelon that consists of political appointments. They often come without any commitment other than promoting their own personal agendas, and the staff is forced to function within those constraints.

After six months of bureaucratic to-and-fro, I realized that the situation was not to my liking, and I sought a return to academia. Fortunately, a suitable opportunity arose back in New York City.

IX

Having been a student at Columbia and a faculty member at NYU, I knew the academic scene in the City but had no experience at any of the numerous schools that form the vast public institution known as The City University of New York. Each of its senior colleges, including such well-known ones as Baruch College, Brooklyn College, City College, Hunter College, and Queens College, offers bachelor's and master's degrees but no doctoral degrees. These are granted only at one school, The Graduate Center, where professors from the constituent colleges come to mid-Manhattan to serve as the faculty in more than thirty fields, and thousands of students are admitted for advanced study. At that time, the school's top administration consisted of a President, a Provost and Vice President for Academic Affairs, and a Dean of Graduate Studies.

I saw an announcement for the Dean's position, and although I knew little about the school, I consulted with friends who assured me I would be a good fit, so I applied. I was interviewed by a group of faculty members with whom I found rapport, and the president, psychologist Harold Proshansky, was someone with whom I felt comfortable. Fortunately, I received an offer, which I was happy to accept. (By this point you might suppose that I invariably was chosen at institutions where I was interviewed, but my record appears so successful only because I am omitting accounts of the numerous instances in which I was not triumphant.)

In any case, a year after I was appointed Dean at the Graduate Center, the position of Provost opened, and I was promoted, thus leading to the most satisfying phase of my career. The school was a center for research, and the faculty and students were serious about the enterprise. Dealing with them was mostly a pleasure, and my work was supported by three people who lightened the administrative load.

First was the Dean for Research, Solomon Goldstein, whose wide knowledge of the sciences, social sciences, and humanities, combined with a puckish sense of humor, made any meeting a delight. He regularly stopped by to chat, offering me much sound advice along with insightful commentary on the passing scene.

Even more central to my everyday life was my Associate Provost Geoffrey Marshall, who arrived shortly after I had assumed my position. He had been Deputy Chairman at the NEH, its highest non-political office. There I had officially reported to him, although at the Graduate Center he officially reported to me. In any case, these bureaucratic distinctions made no difference to us, because we worked together seamlessly. No matter how challenging the situation, Geoffrey approached it with discernment and equanimity. To have his dignified presence by my side was an invaluable source of strength.

Also essential to my administrative efforts was my assistant, Marilyn Marzolf, a former high school Latin teacher, whose acuity, efficiency, and common sense were remarkable. Time and again she provided crucial help and saved me from potential pitfalls.

Most important to any provost, however, is the President, and here again I was lucky. President Proshansky had served as Provost for the founding President, the noted mathematician Mina Rees, who remained the guiding spirit of the institution. After she had been in office for a decade, he succeeded her and stayed for nearly twenty years. He had developed the area of study called environmental psychology and was a shrewd and courageous administrator who in the 1970s had led the school through threats to its existence caused by New York City's financial crisis. He was devoted to the institution's flourishing, having no interest in personal advancement but concerned only with the welfare of the faculty and students. Most days he ate lunch with them in the main dining room, where he kept in close touch with their concerns.

One remarkable feature of his style was that he never allowed his own political commitments to affect his academic decisions. Faculty members, regardless of their points of view, were all treated fairly, and an applicant's political affiliation played no part in appointment or promotion processes.

After we had worked together harmoniously for many years, he suddenly fell ill, and tragically within only a few months he died. For a year I filled in as Acting President, first informally, then formally while a search was undertaken for a successor. At that time the University's rules, subsequently altered, prohibited an Acting President from being considered for the presidency. Thus I knew that accepting the title of Acting President prevented me from being part of the presidential search. I believed, however, that I could not abandon leadership of the Graduate Center while the University was going through threatening times, and indeed spring protests over funding led to students taking over buildings, including ours. We reopened only after days of intense negotiations between me and Geoffrey on one side and the protestors on the other. The disruption was deeply disturbing to many at the Graduate Center, including myself, but eventually the situation calmed without lasting effects.

I asked Geoffrey to keep the incoming President informed of developments, because I wanted the two of them to become better acquainted. After all, new Presidents often prefer to select their own provosts, and therefore I anticipated that I might soon be returning full-time to teaching, an activity I had continued during my service as an administrator. Indeed, when the new President arrived and showed no interest in my staying, I submitted my resignation.

As I had hoped, Geoffrey remained in the administration, first as acting provost, then provost. I believe that he was next in line to become President, a post he would have fulfilled brilliantly, but for me the most unfortunate event in the history of the school was Geoffrey's falling victim at an early age to a fatal illness. With his untimely death my last connection to the administration was severed.

X

Throughout my career I had continued to publish, but shortly after I resumed full-time teaching an unexpected development led to my having a renewed interest in editing anthologies for classroom use. One day I found in my office mailbox a card that had been left by Robert Miller, then a new philosophy editor at Oxford University Press. He had visited, seeking anyone in our Program who might wish to develop textbooks. Given my experience in that sort of endeavor, I had no hesitation contacting him and discussing possible projects.

Previously I had edited for the Hackett Publishing Company a widely-used reader titled *Classics of Western Philosophy*, now in its eighth edition, but Robert was interested not just in one book but in a long-term association that would lead to numerous volumes. Our warm relationship has continued for twenty-five years, resulting in seventeen anthologies, many in multiple editions. I remain grateful for his continuing encouragement and guidance.

Additionally, while along the way I wrote monographs in both philosophy and education, over the past decade I have increased my pace, authoring six books: *From Student to Scholar: A Candid Guide to Becoming A Professor*; *Polishing Your Prose: How* to *Turn First Drafts Into Finished Work* (with my brother, Victor L. Cahn); *Happiness and Goodness: Philosophical Reflections on Living Well* (with Christine Vitrano); *Religion Within Reason; Teaching Philosophy: A Guide*; and *Inside Academia: Professors, Politics, and Policies.*

The first four of these were published by Columbia University Press. Of course, I especially welcomed the opportunity to be associated with the press of my alma mater. But, in addition, its philosophy editor, Wendy Lochner, had encouraged me to submit my work because, as she told me when she introduced herself at an American Philosophical Association meeting, she had taken three courses with me while she was an undergraduate at NYU. She supposed I would not remember her, but I did, and even found her name in one of my old grade books. Her support has been critical to my undertaking such varied projects.

XI

While I pursued my scholarship, I continued to play a role in the Ph.D. Program in Philosophy. I strongly supported its policy of welcoming all qualified applicants and, through core courses and comprehensive examinations, providing graduates with the appropriate background for teaching students at various types of institutions.

The new administration at the Graduate Center, however, urged the Program to alter its goal and concentrate instead on raising its already high national ranking. To help achieve this aim, large sums of money were earmarked, even at a time of budget constraints, to add a sizable number of professors to an already impressive group. Yet while the faculty was expanded, the number of students admitted was dramatically decreased, because exclusivity was thought to enhance reputation. Furthermore, core courses, viewed as simplistic, were dropped, and comprehensive examinations, dismissed as pedantic, were abandoned. In short, all were seen as wasting time that could be better spent on research.

As a result of these changes, the Program became somewhat better known nationally, while its original mission was lost. This transformation was opposed by many of the faculty, including me and my friend David Rosenthal, the outstanding philosopher of mind, but the administration did not share our concerns. Thus the Program, although publicly funded, remains closed to all but a few of the many who apply.

Once I realized that the Program as I had known it was gone, I decided that at age seventy-three I would retire. I did so, as I preferred, without ceremony.

XII

I should not conclude these reminiscences without mentioning the one group that through the years has meant so much to me: my students. They have done more than they know to enhance the sense of satisfaction I have found with my life in academia. While most have disappeared from my view, quite a number have stayed in touch, and six have been my co-author or co-editor on book projects: Maureen Eckert, Tziporah Kasachkoff, Peter J. Markie, David Shatz, Robert B. Talisse, and Christine Vitrano.

Finally, I want to express my appreciation to the two people who have contributed most to whatever success I have enjoyed. First is my brother, Victor L. Cahn, Professor Emeritus of English at Skidmore College, a prolific critic of dramatic literature and a playwright with numerous productions coast to coast (and internationally). Throughout many decades his advice, stylistic and substantive, has been invaluable. Most important has been my wife, Marilyn Ross, MD, to whom I owe more than I would try to express in words.

Sources

UNLESS OTHERWISE NOTED, ALL materials are copyrighted by Steven M. Cahn and can only be used with his permission.

1. *Think* 13.38 (Autumn 2014). Reprinted by permission of the Royal Institute of Philosophy. The postscript was published in *Think* 16.45 (Spring 2017).

2. Published on the APA blog (April 12, 2018) and reprinted with permission.

3. *Philosophy in the Contemporary World* 20:1 (Spring 2013). Reprinted by permission of The Society for Philosophy in the Contemporary World.

4. *Think* 15.44 (Autumn 2016). Reprinted by permission of the Royal Institute of Philosophy.

5. *Think* 16.46 (Summer 2017). Reprinted by permission of the Royal Institute of Philosophy.

6. *Think* 17.49 (Summer 2018). Reprinted by permission of the Royal Institute of Philosophy.

7. Published on the APA blog (January 22, 2018) and reprinted with permission.

8. Published on the APA blog (January 17, 2017) and reprinted with permission.

9. Published on the APA blog (February 26, 2018), and reprinted with permission.

10. Published on the APA blog (May 14, 2018) and reprinted with permission.

11. Published on the APA blog (December 11, 2017) and reprinted with permission.

12. Published on the APA blog (November 14, 2017) and reprinted with permission.

13. Published on the APA blog (October 11, 2018) and reprinted with permission.

14. *Teaching Ethics* 15.2 (Fall 2015). Reprinted with permission of the Society for Ethics Across the Curriculum.

15. *Journal of Social Philosophy* 44.2 (Summer 2013) and reprinted with permission of Wiley Periodicals, Inc.

16. Published here for the first time. Copyright© 2019 by Steven M. Cahn.

BIBLIOGRAPHY

Badhwar, Neera K. *Well-Being: Happiness in a Worthwhile Life.* New York: Oxford University Press, 2014.

Beauchamp, Tom L. "Quotas by Any Name: Some Problems of Affirmative Action in Faculty Appointments." In *Affirmative Action: A Philosophical Inquiry*, edited by Steven M. Cahn. Philadelphia: Temple University Press, 1993.

Blake, William. "Auguries of Innocence." In *William Blake: The Complete Poems*, edited by Alicia Ostriker, 510. London: Penguin, 2004.

Boydston, Jo Ann, ed. *The Middle Works of John Dewey, 1899–1924.* Vol. 9, *Democracy and Education.* Carbondale: Southern Illinois University Press, 1985.

Cahn, Steven M. *Teaching Philosophy: A Guide.* New York: Routledge, 2018.

Cahn, Steven M., and Victor L. Cahn. *Polishing Your Prose: How To Turn First Drafts Into Finished Work.* New York: Columbia University Press, 2013.

Cahn, Victor L. *Walking Distance: Remembering Classic Episodes from Classic Television.* Eugene: OR: Wipf & Stock, 2014.

Darwall, Stephen. *Welfare and Rational Care.* Princeton: Princeton University Press, 2002

Dworkin, Ronald. *Religion Without God.* Cambridge: Harvard University Press, 2013.

Frankfurt, Harry. "Reply to Susan Wolf." In *Contours of Agency: Essays on Themes from Harry Frankfurt*, edited by Sarah Buss and Lee Overton, 250. Cambridge: MIT, 2002.

Glover, Jonathan. *What Sorts of People Should There Be.* New York: Penguin, 1984.

Griffin, James. *Well-Being.* Oxford: Oxford University Press, 2011.

Hume, David. *Dialogues Concerning Natural Religion and Other* Writings. Edited by Dorothy Coleman. Cambridge: Cambridge University Press, 2007.

Hurka, Thomas. *The Best Things in Life: A Guide to What Really Matters.* New York: Oxford University Press, 2011.

Kekes, John. "The Injustice of Strong Affirmative Action." In *Affirmative Action and the University: A Philosophical Inquiry*, edited by Steven M. Cahn. Philadelphia: Temple University Press, 1993.

Kraut, Richard. *What is Good and Why.* Cambridge: Harvard University Press, 2007.

Levy, Neil. "Downshifting and Meaning in Life." *Ratio* 18 (2005) 187–88.

Loxterkamp, Max. "Morality, Objective Value and Living a Meaning Life: A Reply to Steven M. Cahn and Christine Vitrano's Essay 'Living Well.'" *Think* 15.43 (Summer 2016).

Marsden, George M. *Jonathan Edwards: A Life.* New Haven: Yale University Press, 2003.

Nozick, Robert. *Anarchy, State, and Utopia.* New York: Basic, 1974.

———. *The Examined Life: Philosophical Meditations.* New York: Simon & Schuster, 1989.

Robinson, John Manley. *An Introduction to Early Greek Philosophy.* Boston: Houghton Mifflin Company, 1968.

Saltman, Phil. *Method of Modern Jazz Piano Playing.* Rev. ed. Boston: Boston Music Company, 1937.

Schopenhauer, Arthur. "On the Variety and Suffering of Life." In *Happiness: Classic and Contemporary Readings in Philosophy*, edited by Steven M. Cahn and Christine Vitrano. New York: Oxford University Press, 2008.

Sumner, L. W. *Welfare, Happiness, and Ethics.* Oxford: Clarendon, 1999.

Swinburne, Richard. *Is There a God?* Oxford: Oxford University Press, 1996.

Tannajo, Torbjorn. "Narrow Hedonism." *Journal of Happiness Studies* 8:79–98.

Taylor, Richard. *Good and Evil.* Amherst: Prometheus, 2000.

Wolf, Susan. *Meaning in Life and Why It Matters.* Princeton: Princeton University Press, 2010.

ABOUT THE AUTHOR

STEVEN M. CAHN IS Professor Emeritus of Philosophy at the City University of New York Graduate Center, where he served for nearly a decade as Provost and Vice President for Academic Affairs, then as Acting President.

He was born in Springfield, Massachusetts, in 1942. His early years were devoted to the piano, which he studied with Herbert Stessin of the Juilliard School and the renowned chamber music artist Artur Balsam. After earning an AB from Columbia College in 1963 and PhD in philosophy from Columbia University in 1966, his academic career included positions at Dartmouth College, Vassar College, New York University, and the University of Vermont, where he chaired the Department of Philosophy.

He then served as a program officer at the Exxon Education Foundation, as Acting Director for Humanities at the Rockefeller Foundation, and as the first Director of General Programs at the National Endowment for the Humanities. He formerly chaired the American Philosophical Association's Committee on the Teaching of Philosophy, was the Association's delegate to the American Council of Learned Societies, and was longtime President of the John Dewey Foundation. In the latter position he initiated and brought to fruition the John Dewey Lectures, which are now presented at every national meeting of the American Philosophical Association and are delivered by senior philosophers who discuss how their careers were influenced by the people and issues of their times.

Dr. Cahn has authored or edited more than sixty books. His numerous articles have appeared in a broad spectrum of publications, including *The Journal of Philosophy, The Chronicle of Higher Education, Shakespeare Quarterly, The American Journal of Medicine, The New Republic,* and *The New York Times.*

A collection of essays written in his honor, edited by two of his former doctoral students, Robert B. Talisse of Vanderbilt University and Maureen Eckert of the University of Massachusetts Dartmouth, is titled *A Teacher's Life: Essays for Steven M. Cahn.*

Index

Abraham, 35–39
academics. *See also* department, academic
  advice for students within, 64–66
  affirmative action within, 53–59, 75–76
  blackboard and chalk method, 84
  curriculum offerings for, 70
  diversity within, 54–55
  doctoral, 64–66
  doctoral degree within, 67–68
  morality within, 65
  orientation for, 63–66
  politics within, 50
  research *versus* teaching within, 70
  role of professors within, 71
  voting within, 51–52
activities
  experiencing virtual reality of, 18–23
  finding meaning through, 6–8, 10
Adelphi College, 91
advertising, incompleteness in, 75–76
affirmative action
  challenges of, 75–76
  definition of, 53

preferences of, 56–57
purpose of, 54
role of, 59
secrecy within, 57–58
afterlife, 40–44
age, affirmative action within, 54–56
agent-neutral values, 9
agony, escaping through experience machine, 21
Albee, George, 89
alcohol, distorting reality, 19
Alexander the Great, 20
alternate reality, 18–24
altruism, 79–80
American Philosophical Association, 87, 90, 99
Amos, 34–35
ancestors, experiencing the lives of, 20
anger, of God, 39
animals, 10
appearances, 18–23
applicants, affirmative action and, 53
Aristotle, 11, 68
arts, 47–50
atheist, religion of, 3
attitude, toward God, 35–36

Bach, J.S., 47–48
Badhwar, Neera K., 15–16